POTTY TRAINING FOR BOYS

SAY GOOD-BYE TO DIAPERS IN 3 DAYS: STRESS-FREE TODDLER TOILET TRAINING

JANE YORK

CONTENTS

INTRODUCTION

Parents are notoriously competitive. We are all guilty of it, even if it's on a subconscious level. It's natural that we want to show off our child's amazing abilities, and potty training is no different.

Sarah was determined to make sure her little boy mastered this milestone without stress and tears. She had listened to all the usual advice from other parents, but things weren't going as planned. After one successful pee in the potty, she was convinced her son had mastered it!

So, one day while cooking, she was thrilled when her son burst into the kitchen with his pants around his ankles, shouting, "Poop, poop, poop!" Celebrations occurred, the potty song was sung, and the rewards were given. A few minutes later, she went to investigate her son's success and discovered the poop was not in the potty. And if that wasn't bad enough, the robot vacuum had gotten to it first!

Potty training can be a nightmare to navigate. One minute your child seems to have mastered the potty, and the next, you are five steps back. As parents, it's frustrating and heartbreaking to see the disappointment on these little faces, knowing they aren't doing it on purpose.

Even if your child learns to use the potty at home, there is still this fear of accidents in public and what to do when they are sleeping. Ironically, there is a blissful moment between the early months and potty training when it feels like everyone is getting the necessary sleep. But accidents at night lead to parents and children waking up, lacking sleep, and experiencing more stress during the day. All of these challenges can be harder if you are raising your child alone or you have more than one young child.

Some children see the potty as a "big boy" activity and would happily sit on it for half an hour without activity. Others fear the potty and refuse to try, even holding in pee and poo, which can upset their stomachs. Neither of these approaches is ideal.

You have probably invested a lot of time and money on potty training, which is understandable, but there needs to be a limit. You can't keep washing multiple loads of laundry and forking out for the new reward system just to see no results. All the while, people are questioning your approach, offering unsolicited advice, and in better words, "peeing on your confidence."

First things first, there is no judgment here. My two energetic boys presented me with practically every potty-training challenge you can imagine. With my first son, I sensed the critical eyes of others and followed every piece of advice from books, the internet, and those who obviously knew better. As the months went by, my son just didn't seem to get the hang of it. Although potty training isn't a race, as his friends all started to ditch the diapers, I started worrying that something was wrong with him. The pressure increased until I realized I was only causing my son more distress.

Sitting on the floor with an innocent two-year-old and yet another pile of pee, I gave up on everything that hadn't been working for us and started from scratch. I was already passionate about child development and decided to use this to our advantage. I sat up for hours researching the anatomy, techniques, and even the psychology behind potty training.

I didn't begin the process straight away. I had created a 3-day potty training plan, but I wanted to ensure all the conditions were right first. That started with my own attitude.

We then had to find the ideal time between busy schedules. Three days may not sound like much, but with two working parents and other commitments, we both needed to know we could allocate the time.

Why three days? Think about any skill you need to learn. Will your skill develop faster over a matter of weeks or with an intense short course? Some parents think that an intense approach means it's too much for young children, but spreading it out over a longer period can lead to confusion.

We are going to set the potty-training scene first by understanding your little boy's physical and psychological readiness before getting to know their unique challenges. We will move on to a detailed guide for each of the three days before dealing with specific issues and how to make sure you and your little boy are maintaining these positive results, regardless of where you are.

The most important breakthrough I noticed with my son is that my techniques required a combination of practicality and compassion, which is exactly what parents who are going through the same struggles I did need.

Potty training is typically stressful and confusing for parents and the child, but it doesn't have to be. The tried-and-true techniques in *Potty Training for Boys in 3 Days* worked for my boys and dozens of other families I have helped.

My hope now is to extend this method to other parents and turn their potty-training nightmare into a chance for bonding and confidence-building full of celebrations. It won't be easy, but that was evident the moment you became a parent. Still, you have overcome challenges before, and you will again!

There is a difference between intense and rushing, and as much as you want to start day 1, the first place is to check in with your readiness and your child's before beginning.

CHAPTER ONE.
UNDERSTANDING YOUR LITTLE BOY

Many will argue that there shouldn't be a difference between potty training girls and boys, and to an extent, the process is the same. However, you can't ignore one blinding difference in the shape of a penis. In this chapter, we also discuss physiological differences but always respecting the fact that each child is unique and shouldn't be labeled based on gender!

BOYS VS. GIRLS: THE DIFFERENCE

Before delving into the differences between girls and boys, it's crucial to understand that each child is different. No research or personal experience will categorically say that girls are easier to potty train than boys or vice versa. Though studies and statistics can highlight certain points, they will never be able to take into consideration your son's personality. That's not to say that understanding differences doesn't help, but it's not something you should be rigid about.

The first obvious difference is the penis which leads to the sitting or standing debate. For girls, this is much easier because everything is sitting. Parents have to choose between sitting for poo and standing for pee or sitting for both. Most professionals recommend sitting for both (Johns Hopkins Medicine, 2019). This is because standing requires additional developmental skills such as aim. Furthermore, a combination of sitting and standing could lead to more confusion for your child.

Even when sitting, boys still need to learn how to position their penis so that the pee actually makes it into the potty. Some boys may accept sitting on the potty for both; however, if there are older male role models, little boys likely want to do the same. Even if you decide one way is better than the other, it's best to follow the child's lead if they seem to prefer the other. Forcing one method over the other can cause problems.

The less obvious difference is the bladder. For boys, the bladder is between the pubic bone and the rectum. For girls, it sits in front of the vagina and uterus. For adults, this means that women have a lower maximum bladder capacity, but it's a common myth that children share the same problem. The bladder is located in the child's abdomen, so the capacity and frequency to pee aren't gender-based.

It's useful to know that younger children need to pee more frequently. A small bladder can hold around 120 milliliters of urine, increasing by 30 milliliters per year. While I don't recommend obsessing and charting the exact amount of fluid a child drinks, it is useful to be aware of what drinking the average 120 to 200 milliliter juice box can do.

Aside from the physiological differences, the psychological differences between potty training boys and girls are the main influential factor. Boys generally start later. One study showed that 56 percent of girls were daytime trained by 2.5 years old compared with 44 percent of boys (Vethavanam, 2023).

The theory behind the age of readiness, even though it may only be a few months, is that girls and boys tend to learn in different ways. Boys often focus on one activity for a short time and then switch to a different one, whether a puzzle or potty training. They also prefer more space for learning new activities and more movement. Girls find it easier to concentrate on one activity for a longer period and in smaller spaces.

Labeling boys such as "they are slower to mature" is wrong, as this is not the case. A lot of the success of potty training also comes down to communication, a skill that girls develop faster than boys. Girls not only pick up vocabulary more quickly but also develop gestures earlier.

There are other differences to consider, but not concerning gender. Different cultures will take different approaches to potty training. In Kenya, Vietnam, and Iran, parents look for signs of pee and poo as babies, even newborns. When babies show signs, parents hold them over a toilet or similar object. Whereas in China, parents favor split-crotch pants over diapers, and there is no need for them to lower their pants, making the process easier. The significant difference between these cultures and the West is that we tend to wait for signs of readiness.

One rather bizarre correlation is the link between potty training and latitude. Children who live closer to the equator tend to be potty trained earlier than those who live in colder climates. Pediatrician Dr. Sydney Spiesel has noticed this correlation but also recognized that it hasn't been studied yet (Howard, 2017).

HOW IS YOUR MINDSET?

Even months before potty training, parents start to dread what will come, and with good reason. It requires patience, it's messy, and it's unpredictable. This is not the right way to begin, though! It's possible to notice that even young children pick up on adult emotions. When parents are angry, it's common to see increased tension in children. This is known as emotional transference.

Before you begin potty training with your son, you need to change your mindset from one that assumes it will be a terrible time in your life to one where you are positively helping your child develop their skills—and without faking that smile!

It's a good idea to use positive affirmations to encourage the right mindset prior to starting out. Some examples include:

- I trust myself to do what is best for my child's education.
- I am a loving, patient, safe space for my child.
- I am so proud of my children.
- Our environment is safe, loving, and a great place to learn.

Because the adult mindset is a crucial part of the 3-day potty training for boys method, chapter 14 is dedicated to the parent's mindset and approach. Nevertheless, it needs a conscious effort from parents from the get-go.

TAPPING INTO HIS MINDSET

The first question parents want to ask is what age to start potty training boys. Research suggests that two years old (Kiddoo, 2012) is the ideal age because they are keen to learn new skills without power struggles, and their brains are developed enough to recognize signs and understand what is happening to their body. However, it's absolutely fine if they start potty training later. The better question is, are you both ready?

Family readiness must be considered. For example, any situations that increase stress levels in the home indicate that it's not a good time. This can include new siblings, moving home, divorce, or family illness.

Parents need to be fully committed because potty training can be intense. Being a full-time working mom, I knew this was my greatest challenge before choosing the right time to start. To make the process easier, I decided to start on a weekend with a public holiday so that my husband and I were both off, and I scheduled a couple of extra vacation days afterward just to be on the safe side. This isn't always possible, and if that's the case, find yourself a potty-training buddy, someone you trust will follow your directions precisely, and someone your son trusts too.

Signs of readiness can be classified as developmental or potty-specific.

Developmental Signs

- **There are signs of communication:** This doesn't mean words. Communication can be in the signs of gestures, sign language, or visual support.

- **The ability to follow simple directions:** Ideally, your child should be able to follow two-step directions such as "Can you pick up your teddy and put it in the toy box?"

- **He can copy gestures:** Again, the signs don't have to be complicated and can be simple gestures like typing on a computer or putting laundry away. If they can copy these actions, it will be easier for them to copy your positive examples in the bathroom.

- **He is eager to please:** Positive reinforcement is the best way to work with children and potty training. If there aren't signs of willingness to please, it will be harder to motivate them with rewards.

- **He has good gross motor skills:** These skills include things like sitting, standing, and walking. On the one hand, these skills are essential for safety. On the other hand, they will be exceptionally convenient. After success, you want to celebrate and not have to worry about wobbly legs.

- **He can pull his pants and underwear down:** This will help prevent accidents and a feeling of shame that might begin to develop at this age.

Potty Specific Signs

- **He is interested in the toilet:** Toddlers love to follow you everywhere and more so in the bathroom, but make sure they are curious about the actual toilet and not just following you for company.

- **He is staying dry for longer:** A good rule of thumb is to make sure that they are staying dry for at least an hour during the day. You may also notice that you don't need to change their diaper as often.

- **There are poop patterns:** While there is so much focus on pee, don't forget the poop signs. Rather than focusing on frequency, look for signs of certain times of the day.

- **There are clean nap diapers:** If your son wakes up from nap time and the diaper is clean, this is a good readiness sign. Remember that night times will need different expectations and often won't happen until potty training begins.

- **He hides his pooping:** If your child takes himself away and returns with a dirty diaper, this is an excellent sign because they are learning to recognize the signs of needing to go.

- **There are visible signs:** Your child may fidget, cross their legs, or pull recognizable faces. Some children may tell you when they are going.

- **He asks for a diaper change:** Another excellent sign is when they ask you to change their diaper, whether it's wet or dirty. This indicates that they are uncomfortable, making it easier to encourage them to start using the potty.

Even though there are signs of readiness, it doesn't mean that your little boy won't experience anxiety when it comes to potty training. After all, it's a new experience for him.

Despite being interested in what happens in the bathroom, it doesn't mean that there will be fear at the first signs of potty, and this can't be mistaken for laziness or toddler defiance.

This fear of potty training can be exacerbated if a child has suffered from any physical problem such as constipation or the smaller risk of urinary tract infections. Medical conditions involving pee and poop may lead to children associating the potty with pain.

A common mistake many parents make (myself included) is to see signs of fear and assume their son isn't ready for potty training. They will wait a few months and then start again. In that time, developmental skills and readiness might improve, but the moment the potty reappears, the fear is back!

To overcome and prevent potty anxiety, it's advisable to introduce the potty before you begin the 3-day intense training. Begin by having the potty in visible locations but don't necessarily bring too much attention to it. Once the initial nerves subside, you can encourage your son to sit on the potty, not for any results, just to sit for a few minutes and allow them to get used to this new experience. Clothes should remain on at this point, and try to limit the time from 30 seconds to 1 minute.

After each success, there should be plenty of praise, but if your child doesn't want to sit on the potty, provide a lot of reassurance. Use phrases like "It's okay, we can try again later" or "The most important thing is that you tried." Don't forget to check in with your body language and tone of voice to match the message you want your child to hear.

One of my absolute favorite ways to overcome potty anxiety is through the use of social stories. Social stories were the creation of Carol Gray as a way of helping autistic children and adults navigate difficult situations. Today, they are widely used by professionals, from speech and language therapists to play therapists.

Essentially, a social story is a breakdown of an activity you would like to accomplish with a child. In terms of potty training, there would be a simple story of a character performing the steps to potty training, such as:

1. Going to the bathroom
2. Pulling down their pants
3. Pulling down their underwear
4. Sitting on the potty
5. Wiping
6. Pulling up their underwear
7. Pulling up their pants
8. Flushing the pee/poop
9. Washing hands

Download Potty Training Social Story

Each step is presented on an individual page, with a simple sentence and often an image. There are numerous free potty training social stories that you can download and print, like the one in the resource below.

I prefer to make my **own social stories** because I can personalize them to engage my boys. I downloaded images of the steps for my first son and wrote a sentence with his name in the story. If you can't print images, drawing simple stick figures is good.

For my second son, I managed to get some photos of him doing different steps (except for sitting and flushing), but I used these photos, and it was lovely to see that enthusiasm on his face that we had been missing before.

Finally, let's discuss some genuine ways to motivate little boys to start wanting to use the potty—after all, the goal is for them to use a potty because they want to, not because they are being forced to.

Begin by choosing a potty that they will love. You may want to let them pick one out or at least choose a specific color. You can use a permanent marker to write their name on it and add some drawings or encourage them to decorate it with stickers.

It's also wise to have a special book, toy, or both that are exclusive for potty time. Let them play with the toy as soon as they sit on the potty, even with their clothes on. I found it helpful to have an egg timer next to the potty so that my boys knew when it was time to hand back the toy or book. Make sure they don't see the removal of this special activity as a punishment and keep it close to the potty so that they associate the toy with potty time.

The big boy pants are what this huge rite of passage is for a toddler. This is a chance for them to connect with their favorite characters and choose the underwear that they want to wear. I can't stress this enough: if they don't get to choose the underwear that makes them feel special, where is the motivation?

This could be Spidey, dinosaurs, tigers or their favorite sports team! Even if you're not a big fan of some characters on their clothes, what's most important is how happy it makes your child.

Now that we understand our boys, let's prepare the battleground for a successful potty-training experience, focusing especially on a more detailed look at the supplies you will need!

By the way, there's more for you on the next page – including the downloadable checklist and additional resources!

GET YOUR FREE POTTY TRAINING CHECKLIST

Dear Reader,

I'm thrilled you picked my book for your son's potty training. It's a big step, and I am here to make it easier and more fun for both of you.

As my way of saying thanks, I've prepared a Free Potty Training Checklist for you. It's a simple resource to help you through the potty training process with handy tips and milestones.

What's Inside :

- Action Steps Checklist for Every Day of Potty Training
- Free Resources and Tools
- Recommendations and Supplies

How to Access Your Free Checklist

Simply scan the QR code with your smartphone or tablet, and you'll be directed to the checklist page.

Get Your Free Checklist Here

Use it on your device, or download and print it out, and let the potty training adventure begin!

Thank you once again for trusting me to be a part of this special time in your child's development.

If you have any difficulty downloading the checklist, contact me at **janeyorkauthor@gmail.com**, and I'll send you a copy as soon as possible.

CHAPTER TWO. PREPARING FOR THE BIG THREE DAYS

It's tempting to dash out and get that potty, but I promise you, that laying the foundations and making sure that everyone involved is prepared will make the next three days and beyond go a lot smoother.

CHOOSING THE RIGHT TIME

As mentioned in the previous chapter, potty training must begin at the right time. Many parents who have achieved success believe that the most important factor in success is making sure parents are free to commit to the process, rather than the age of the child. To illustrate this, let's examine two different case studies.

Indy

Indy had recently moved to a new house with her partner, and her son had just turned two years old. For Indy, it made sense to start potty training as soon as they arrived in the new house, as the potty could be introduced, and she wanted her son to learn how big boys go to the toilet in the new house. She took pride in her organizational skills and wasn't expecting any major stress. Additionally, she and her partner had both taken time off for the move, so she felt more confident that she would have time to help her son.

But this was the first time she had moved house with a toddler, and needless to say, there was a lot to do, and it was more stressful than she realized. Initially, potty training seemed to start well. Indy had already noticed signs of her son being ready and they even had some successful pees on the potty. This early success, combined with their busy schedule, meant both parents weren't paying enough attention. A handful of accidents and Indy's emotions got the better of her. Indy's partner felt that their son wasn't ready, which only caused Indy to think there was something wrong with her son.

Potty training was on hold off for a few months. Indy learned that it wasn't enough to be at home. She had to make sure that both parents were available and not occupied by other tasks.

Billie

Billie and his partner were expecting their second child, and they thought it would make sense to start potty training their son before the baby came along. As his wife was still working and struggling with the pregnancy, Billie decided it would primarily be his role to potty train. He had a 4-day week coming up, so this would be the ideal time. What he hadn't factored in was that although he wasn't working, he was still on call, and as luck would have it, he was called out several times. Potty training wasn't completed that weekend and Billie was upset that his schedule had led to a more challenging experience.

Don't get me wrong, it's not like you need to spend three entire days doing nothing but watching your little boy. That's simply not practical.

But you should find a weekend with no other responsibilities that will distract you from the end goal.

I found this to be a great time to get a load of those "sit down" jobs that always seem to get put off; the ones that tend to take less than half an hour but there is never half an hour free. Treat it as a staycation!

And let's be realistic: dedicating an entire three days solely to your son may not be possible, or it may not fit into the time frame you had hoped for beginning potty training. This doesn't mean that the 3-day potty training isn't possible.

If this is your situation, the best thing is to try and make sure your son is at home for the majority of the three days and those that are with him are fully aware of the potty-training plan and, in the perfect world, are as committed as you are.

GATHERING ESSENTIAL SUPPLIES

The type of potty is the biggest decision to make when shopping for supplies. This may depend on your budget, and you may have had recommendations from other parents.

If you have multiple bathrooms, make sure you have the same option for each bathroom to prevent confusion.

The following list describes different potty types. You will also find the pros and cons of each.

Permanent Toilet Seat

The first choice is a permanent toilet seat, which is basically the same as a standard seat that flips down but smaller.

Pros: It takes up no extra space.

Cons: It's not the safest option as a stool will be needed.

Removable Toilet Seat

There is also the option of a removable toilet seat, which is a smaller version of a standard seat but sits on top.

Pros: Children can easily put the seat on themselves, and it's one of the cheaper options.

Cons: They will still need a stool.

A Potty

The traditional potty is cost-effective and easy to use. There are so many options, from cheap and cheerful to fun potties.

You may want to consider a portable potty for after the initial three days if you are an active family.

Pros: Highly convenient and safe.

Cons: Some children might find it difficult to switch from the potty to a toilet, which doesn't help when you aren't at home.

2-in-1 Options

A 2-in-1 toilet seat with a stool avoids the issue of having to buy a seat and stool. They are removable and sit over a normal toilet.

Pros: Boys can start using a toilet straight away and in a safe way as there are only one or two small steps and handles.

Cons: It takes up floor space and some children might not be able to position it themselves.

Aside from choosing a potty that matches your needs, my advice is to make sure it has a built-in splash guard. This splash guard will prevent pee from spilling on the outside of the toilet, and anything that reduces cleaning at this stage is a worthy investment. Speaking of which, an easy-to-clean potty is also helpful!

Explore potty training supplies deals and free resources in your checklist. Scan the QR code to get it on your phone

---

Underwear

Next on the shopping list will be underwear. While your little boy needs to be the one choosing things like color and design, you will have to decide which type. Pull-ups are all the rage, but experts advise against them. The only difference is that they pull on like underwear. At the end of the day, they have the same or similar absorbency to diapers. Real underwear lets toddlers feel when they are wet and although this sounds cruel, the discomfort of feeling wet encourages them to use the potty.

Another option is training pants. These are special underwear that are more absorbent than regular underwear. Using training pants can make things a little less messy, but children still feel wet. They are washable, so you will still save money compared to diapers.

On the other hand, going straight into underwear can promote that feeling of independence that motivates so many young children. We started with regular underwear because we were only expecting accidents for a few days, but it's a personal decision. Either way, buy more than you think you will need!

Making Things Fun

The last thing on my list brought more fun into the process. Understandably, their hand-eye coordination is a skill little boys need and takes time to develop, which isn't always fun for you! There are some great potty-training targets available. One type is a laser that attaches to the inside of the lid and sends out a beam into the bowl.

Others are paper targets coming in a wide range of images. Your little boy needs to throw one in the toilet and aim. The paper then disintegrates.

Attention! There Is No Need to Spend Money on Making Things Fun!

Whether it's targets on tissue paper or your own reward chart, you can use this opportunity to get creative and make your own pity-training items together with your son. Not only is this a way to spend quality time together while developing skills, but it's also a chance to engage them further in the potty-training process.

Progress Charts

There are dozens to choose from, and it's something your child can pick out on their own. You can choose from dinosaurs, animals, or simple star charts. The idea of each is the same—stickers for each success. It's great if you can choose one that has separate rewards for pee and poop.

Others come with additional extras like stickers to help children follow the steps and diplomas. I particularly like the following option for the sticker under the toilet roll so they know how much to pull!

Cleaning Supplies

There is no getting around this—you will need additional cleaning supplies. I am all about saving the planet and choosing eco-friendly options but not for these few days. I made sure there was a decent supply of multipurpose cleaning wipes that cleared up any mess in a matter of seconds. While looking for wipes, include flushable wipes for your little boy. It's another item that makes the process special for him in the beginning.

I hope I'm not alone in getting excited by new cleaning products. To add a little smile to my face when accidents happen, I made sure I had a few new products to try, as well as the faithful favorites. If you have carpets, don't forget a fabric cleaner, which will come in handy for sofas too.

Cleaning hands can't be forgotten. There are many types of soap dispensers available, including fun and automatic animal-shaped ones that my boys loved.

Basic Comfort Tips

Double-check that all of their clothes are comfortable, loose-fitting, and easy to pull up and down. Buttons and zips are not your friends! You will also want to add extra bedding and a waterproof mattress cover to your list. Even though nighttime training doesn't start at the same time, it's best to have things ready.

SETTING UP THE BATHROOM

Once you have the essential supplies, it's time to create a safe and encouraging environment. If your bathroom has the room, it's great to set aside a space close to the toilet but just for them. Scan the area and make sure there is nothing they could hurt themselves on, bump heads on, or trap fingers in.

It goes without saying that safety is crucial to prevent injuries because aside from hurting themselves, they could also start fearing the potty. But safety should also allow you to give them some privacy. Knowing that they are safe, you can turn away or even leave the room for a short period of time. There are an estimated 20 million people in the US affected by shy bladder (Nall, 2018), and it can occur at any age, including toddlers!

If you choose a type of potty that requires a stool, it's advisable to place it next to a wall for added safety. This wall will also be handy for keeping track of your child's potty progress on a chart.

YOUR 3-DAY POTTY TRAINING CHECKLIST

Let's summarize these first two chapters with a checklist of what will make the 3-day potty training method run smoothly!

- A potty/seat/stool
- Underwear/training pants
- Potty training chart
- Potty training targets
- Flushable wipes
- Hand wash
- Special potty toy/book
- Timer
- Potty training-friendly clothes

- Extra bedding
- Multipurpose wipes
- Cleaning productsWith our schedule organized, our mindsets prepared and positive, and the space ready, it's time to delve into the nitty-gritty of the 3-day method!

CHAPTER THREE. DAY 1: LAYING THE FOUNDATION

MORNING RITUALS

It's going to be an intense day for your son and for you. You will spend an entire day indoors, and your eyes will constantly be on your little one. Bear this in mind the day before. Make sure you have all the essentials and have completed all errands. Start your day in the most positive way. Get up a little earlier and enjoy a shower, coffee, or other rituals that put you at ease.

Before the first day, you will already have done lots of potty awareness, and on the night before, it's a good idea to put them to bed and let them know that the next day is the big "potty day."

If you haven't chosen your potty song, it's a good idea to choose one before your son wakes up. Even the days leading up to it can be helpful for earlier preparation. At the time, my son was going through a Cocomelon phase, so it was the natural choice for us because we liked the potty dance, so we used the lines "When you get that funny feeling way down low, just stop what you're doing and go, go, go!"

Listen to the Cocomelon Potty Training Song

As soon as your little one wakes up, you are going to break out into your potty dance, take off their diaper, and let them try. It doesn't matter if there is no pee or poop.

The success is having them sit on the potty. Tell them they have done a good job and tell them to let you know if they need to use the potty.

Now, you have two options, both advocated by professionals.

Option one is to go straight for the big-boy underwear. The advantage is that they learn the discomfort of having pee and poop in their underwear, but pulling down underwear is a skill, and in the case of potty training, every second counts.

Option two is to go naked, or at least bottomless (with socks if you have cold floors). Some experts suggest that having underwear can create a similar sensation to wearing diapers, which they won't recognize the difference. Ultimately, deciding what's best for your son is up to you.

If you have ever heard someone telling you about how they quit smoking, they may have told you about throwing away all of their cigarettes—it's ceremonial! You can do the same with the diapers. Let your son throw them out and make a big deal of it.

Aside from the ceremonial ditching of the diapers, the early morning potty dance, and the naked bottom, the rest of the morning should look like any other as children thrive on routine. Let them do what they would normally do. The only difference is that you will watch them like a hawk!

RECOGNIZING THE SIGNS

Putting your son on the potty as soon as they wake up makes sense because most people need the toilet first thing in the morning. After that, it's about reminders and reading the signs.

One potty training method requires taking your toddler to the potty and sitting them on it at set intervals, often beginning with 30-minute intervals and extending this to one hour and then two. This approach has its advantages. There will be fewer accidents and more opportunities to celebrate success. But there is a reason why this parent-led approach doesn't combine well with the 3-day approach.

Needless to say, if you are putting your little boy on the potty every 30 minutes, there will likely be pee and the chance of poop, but his bladder may not be completely full. When this happens, his body won't receive the signal that his bladder is full.

While the idea of fewer accidents might be appealing, accidents are necessary for your child to feel uncomfortable and encourage him to use the potty. Furthermore, you don't get to identify the signs of readiness, and on a practical level, if they go to any form of childcare, it's unlikely that the caregiver will be able to place them on the potty with such frequency.

At the same time, we all know how engrossed toddlers can get in their activities, and it will likely be too late for them to stop what they are doing to make it to the potty, even with a bare bum! I remember constantly asking my first son if he needed to go, and in the end, he must have thought I was a little crazy. Nobody wants to hear the same question 40 times a day!

Throughout the day, use gentle reminders about using the potty. Say things like "Let mommy or daddy know if you want to use the potty" (or whoever is responsible). If you go to the bathroom, you could ask if they want to accompany you. Again, it's a positive result if they sit there for a few minutes, even if nothing comes out.

Even if your little boy is using words, sounds, or visual cues, it still might not be early enough to get them to the potty. Though you will have your eye on them all the time, pay extra attention approximately one hour after they have had a large drink. As each child is different, you may notice that it's more like 45 minutes or even 1.5 hours, but you will discover a pattern soon.

Physical signs that they need to pee include crossing their legs, holding their crotch, fidgeting, or performing what is often known as "the pee dance." In these cases, lead by example and go to the toilet together. Signs for poop might be different. You may recognize certain facial expressions indicating they are ready to go, but another sign is passing wind!

Tommy used a few words, but despite his parents' efforts, he wouldn't give any vocal cues when he needed the potty. His parents had spotted the signs of pee, and there had been a success, but poop was still an issue. After extremely close observation, they noticed that Tommy would stop making eye contact and begin to turn around when he needed to poop. Eye contact is a common sign, but the turning around wasn't in any book they had read. As soon as the parents recognized Tommy's unique signs, they were able to get him onto the potty, and there were no more accidents.

CELEBRATING SMALL WINS

The ultimate goal on day 1 is to get some pee and poop in the potty. At first, you might not make it! It's hard to imagine a parent who has not picked up their toddler mid-pee and raced to the potty. Yes, you will have a trail of pee to clean up, but if a few drops of pee make it into that potty, it's time to dance!

Children thrive on positive reinforcement. Despite the tantrums and defiant "no," nothing makes a young child happier than seeing their parents with a proud smile. Whether you choose hugs, kisses, or high-fives, they have to see this as a genuine big deal.

Use your words as well. Say things like, "Look, you did it! Pee/poop goes in the potty" or "You did such an amazing job." Check your tone of voice and ensure there is a level of excitement too.

There is much debate about what time rewards should be used to encourage potty use. Candies or other sweet treats are common, and while I certainly don't judge those who use candy, I'm not in favor of it for a couple of reasons.

On day 1, you should reward your little boy for each correct step, so this could be getting some pee/poop in the potty, wiping, flushing (or at least helping), and washing hands.

That's four sweets every time you go to the bathroom, which amounts to a lot of sugar. I'm also not a huge fan of encouraging food in the bathroom.

I do, however, love stickers. We had a sticker chart on the wall in the bathroom, and I gave a sticker after each correct step.

After a while, the stickers weren't going to motivate them to the same extent, so I made sure that after a certain amount of stickers, there was a slightly bigger reward. In this case, you could use candy or a healthy snack they love. They may also have a favorite type of trinket or collection. If a child loves building bricks, they can collect a new brick for each success.

Much like the signs, it's about finding that unique motivation for your child.

HANDLING ACCIDENTS

No pressure here, but how you handle the inevitable mishaps can make or break potty training success. Always remember that even though it's intense, it's still a learning process and the way we learn is through mistakes, or in this case, accidents. Try to view accidents this way.

When toddlers have an accident, not only do they learn it's uncomfortable, but they are also learning the physical signs their body is telling them, how long they can hold their bladder, and even skills like how long it takes to get to the potty.

One of the biggest fears many parents have is psychologically scarring their child. We don't want them to feel guilt or shame, so instead, we tell them that it's okay. Contrary to popular belief, this is not what we should be saying. By using the word okay, we unintentionally let them know that peeing or pooing in underwear or on the floor is acceptable. Depending on a child's personality, they may even interpret the word "okay" as permission.

That doesn't mean there is no room for reassurance. Try phrases like "Oops, it looks like you peed/pooped on the floor," "Pee and poop only go in the potty," or "You are learning and can try again next time." Support your words with a kind reassuring smile. Your toddler can only see you being calm! If it means walking away and taking your frustration out elsewhere, there is nothing wrong with that; in fact, it's better than bottling it up.

You might be familiar with the law of averages phrase: every no leads you closer to a yes. Perfectly adaptable for potty training, every accident leads you closer to success!

After the inevitable accidents come the inevitable clean-up! Clean up any poop or pee with toilet paper before disinfecting the area. You can use a mixture of vinegar and baking soda, which will disinfect but not to the same extent as commercial cleaners. Another option is a mixture of 1 part bleach to 9 parts water if you don't have disinfectant wipes.

Sofas and carpets need a little more attention. Club soda can be dabbed onto pee, then left to dry before sprinkling with baking soda. After a couple of hours, vacuum the baking soda off. For poop, it's best to use something like oxygen bleach or something similar that is suitable for fabrics. I also found that antibacterial essential oils did a great job of helping with smells. You can try adding a few drops of mint or tea tree to water and spray it on the area.

For potty cleaning, after ditching the pee or poop, rinse with warm water and then disinfect it. During the day, I would use a homemade solution of vinegar, baking soda, lemon juice, and essential oils because I wasn't too keen on harsh chemicals. That being said, I would use bleach in the evening for a thorough cleaning. Don't forget to wipe the floor around the potty, just in case of splashes.

The next question is what to do at night. Nap times are short, so a potty trip before and after is wise, and either underwear or naked while they sleep. Nights are a little trickier. You typically wouldn't expect them to stay dry at night just yet. However, if you have ceremoniously thrown out the diapers, you can't go back now!

This is where pull-up pants might come in handy, or if you notice a small amount of pee in their diapers, you could use training pants. Don't be surprised if your toddler suddenly refuses to wear a diaper at night—hence the extra bedding!

END OF DAY REVIEW

By the end of the first day, many children will have had some success. Your intense observation and frequent reminders may have encouraged them to start vocalizing their needs or using gestures, and something would have ended up in the potty!

If this hasn't happened, do not fret! Some children don't get it until day 2 or even day 3. The most important thing is that you are going in the right direction.

Once your little one is nicely tucked up in bed and all signs of disinfectant are out of sight, take a moment to reflect on the day. It's not just a learning opportunity for toddlers. Many parents are amazed by what they discover on day 1, especially in a fast-paced world that gives them few moments to be with their children.

Consider what went well and give yourself a pat on the back. Don't dwell on the things that didn't go quite as you had planned. Decide what you can learn from these moments and commit to implementing positive changes for day 2. And don't forget, you are a third of the way through already!

Day 1 is done! Let's build on that foundation and tackle day 2.

CHAPTER FOUR. DAY 2: BUILDING CONSISTENCY

You are one-third of the way through. You probably learned a lot about your little one and enjoyed spending quality time with them. However, there may be some dread at the thought of cleaning up accidents the next day. Use day 1 as a learning opportunity and don't assume you're destined for the same experience.

REINFORCEMENT TECHNIQUES

Day 2 should start the same way as day 1, but you might need extra reinforcements! The first day is often the hardest, especially if you haven't had as much success as you had hoped. For some reason, we subconsciously set unreasonable expectations, like our sons are going to master the potty by day 1 and, of course, wake up dry!

From a psychological point of view, you may also feel a little claustrophobic, particularly if you aren't used to spending an entire day at home. Regardless of how you are feeling, your son needs the same enthusiasm as the previous day, so make sure you get up early and have that necessary time to prepare yourself mentally. As you probably spent most of the previous day playing with their toys, you might want to consider some different activities, such as hand painting or baking. Reframe the thought of spending another day at home to a positive one where you have the chance to bond with your little one.

When considering your mentality, don't feel that you are a hostage in your own home. At some point, your son will have to venture out and put his potty-training skills into practice in the real world. If you want to make a short trip to the park or even just a walk around the block, go for it. Just be sure to put them on the potty first or time it after they have had a pee. For poop, you probably know more or less the time of day it's likely to happen.

Once again, I cannot stress the importance of routine, and it helps to understand how your little one's brain is working. When we learn a new skill, regardless of age, neurons in the brain fire together and create a connection called a neural pathway or synapse. The more often the skill is repeated, the stronger the connection becomes and the easier it is to retrieve from our memories.

On day 1, imagine you sang a particular potty song. Each time he heard it, the neurons fired and wired together, and a meaningful connection between the song and needing the potty was made. If you change the song on day 2, the brain needs to create a new neural pathway. The same would occur if you made any change to their routine.

This is the same way positive affirmations work. When you repeat a phrase over and over again, the connection becomes stronger, so much so that the brain starts to believe that your affirmation is true. Day 2's reinforcement technique for you is to repeat a simple phrase such as "We've got this!"

In terms of reinforcements for little ones, you may also need to up your game. After all, only a few people tend to become unimpressed with something rather quickly.

That's not to say that stickers won't still work, but on the second day, you may want to bring out some shiny stickers or stickers of their favorite characters.

Much of day 2 will depend on the progress in day 1. Excluding the poop for a moment, if your son had several successes the previous day and day 2 seems to be going well, you might want to add underwear if you had started off bottomless.

If the success continues, it's also time to reconsider the rewards. No matter what, your praise and enthusiasm must remain at an all-time high, but you can't continue to hand out stickers for each step.

You could, for example, have a special sticker for each completed success, and after three or four stickers, they get a bigger reward.

If there is any sign of disappointment at a change in rewards, return to the previous method and give them more time to adapt.

You may also want to give them the sticker and allow them to stick it on their chart as an extra reward. It might not sound like much to you, but it is for them.

The trick with rewards is to start small so that you know you have room for greater motivation if needed. Why break out the stickers if they are over the moon with your praise?

Rewards don't always have to be tangible. Some children might prefer an extra story, more time on their bike, or a playdate with a friend.

Robbie and Jane were determined not to use candy as a reward for their son. On day 1, they used stickers and were unsuccessful.

On day 2, they used sultanas (knowing their son could safely eat them), but still no pee or poop in the potty. As day 2 came to an end, they both noticed that their stress levels were hitting an all-time high.

They had two options: start day 3 and hope for progress, knowing that they weren't as mentally motivated as they needed to be, or they could resort to candy as the best way to motivate him.

Jane went to the store to buy supplies, and they both went to bed feeling that day 3 would be a new day. As it turned out, that was the day their son had his first pee in the potty!

INCORPORATING FUN ACTIVITIES

Picture this scenario: you are convinced your son needs the potty, so you take him to the bathroom. He sits down for only a few seconds before shaking his head and returning to his toys. Five minutes later, he pees on the floor.

There needs to be a balance between not sitting on the potty for too long and sitting long enough for something to occur. The time limit you should set is five minutes, but if your son gets off the potty before this, you can't punish him. What you can do is find fun ways to encourage him to stay until their timer goes off. Here are some ideas to make potty time fun:

•**The potty doll/action figure:** Have a special doll with their own potty. When your son goes to the potty, he can take their character to the potty and follow the steps, reinforcing the learning.

• **Bubbles:** This is one of my favorites because blowing bubbles helps relax the pelvic floor muscles.

• **Special markers:** If you have tiled walls, dry-erase markers are good fun to let your child color the walls. Draw a large square on the wall so that they learn this is the only area they can color walls. The bonus with coloring is that they are also practicing their fine motor skills.

•**Mini basketball:** Have a special small soft ball that they can practice throwing into the trash can or draw a goal or target on the tiled wall and have them roll the ball to hit the goal or target.

• **Potty treasure hunt:** Hide a couple of their favorite toys in the bathroom and have them look for them while they are sitting on the potty. Let them know they can have the toys once the timer has finished.

• **Make a rainbow:** Get some different colored sticky notes. Each time they are on the potty, they use one color to make a rainbow. Each time they go, they can watch their rainbow grow.

On top of these ideas, you will still have their special potty toy or book. Don't feel you need to have all the activities ready because you may end up overwhelming both of you. If you find one that grabs their attention, stick to it and change the activity when you notice them becoming restless. As with the special potty toy or book, keep these activities for the bathroom only and for this select time; otherwise, they will no longer be special potty activities.

POTTY TRAINING STORIES

Speaking of special potty stories, let's look at some of the best books your little boy will love.

• ***P Is for Potty!* (Sesame Street):** This is a study book that is a good size for 1- to 3-year-olds to hold. It's sturdy and has lots of flaps to lift and explore.

• ***Daniel Tiger's Potty Time!*:** From the Daniel Tiger Neighborhood series, the board book allows children to press the interactive buttons with a potty song, a flush, and handwashing icons.

• ***Dino Potty*:** This cute book follows a rhyming, step-by-step guide for children to follow along.

• ***Potty (Leslie Patricelli board books):*** This incredibly simple book with short sentences that follow the character's inner dialogue, encouraging children to answer the questions as they read along.

• ***Potty Superhero: Get Ready for Big Boy Pants!:*** This story shares how every superhero needs to use the potty. This hero is accompanied by his superhero dog.

Find all book links and free resources in your checklist. Scan the QR code to get it on your phone

There are so many potty-training books, so it shouldn't be difficult for you to find one that uses the same keywords you have been using. For instance, if you say "pee," try not to use a book that uses "wee."

On day 2, you will have some opportunities to take photos of your son doing each step of the process. Now is the perfect time to turn these photos into a personalized potty-training book for your little one! You could even get creative and add a superhero cape if that motivates them more.

Jackson and his son turned potty time into an epic playtime, adding each visit to their adventure. For a few weeks, Jackson had been saving up toilet rolls. Every successful step his son made on day 1 led to a new toilet roll being glued to the last until they had a mini fort by the middle of the second day. From there, his son would take different characters, crayons, and stickers to decorate the fort and create stories around it. The fort remained long after potty training. Jackson was pleased with how easily his son learned and was happy he didn't have to spend a fortune on rewards.

DAY 2 TROUBLESHOOTING

One of the biggest problems that can occur on day 2 is that there are still more accidents than you were hoping for. The first thing to do is double-check you are as eagle-eyed as you were on the first day. It's possible that you may have seen a couple of successful potty trips and now aren't as frequent with your reminders. Set an alarm on your phone for reminders (but please don't use the alarm as a signal for your child).

Another problem is with expectations, especially if day 1 has gone well. It can almost feel like you have gone back a step. The ultimate goal is to have some pee in the potty. Even on day 2 and if need be, on day 3, carry your child to the potty mid-pee so that some ends up in the potty, reinforcing this is where pee and poo need to go and providing a chance for celebration.

One thing I have noticed, and not just with my child but with others as well, is that some children are genuinely afraid of the flush. There could be two main reasons for this. They don't want the flush to take away what they ultimately see as theirs, or they are afraid they will also be flushed away. Their fears may seem irrational to you, but they should be treated with respect and not dismissed. When has someone telling you not to be silly about your fear ever really helped?

If your son shows genuine fear of the flush, extra patience may be required. Move the potty further away from the toilet if possible so that there is a little distance between them. The best way to handle this fear is through gradual exposure. They might feel happier standing by the door while you flush. As their anxiety increases, have them take a couple of steps closer, again waiting for the signs of anxiety to decrease before a few more steps.

It's common for parents to face resistance on day 2. Their child simply refuses to use the potty altogether, or they might pee in the potty but will refuse to poop. I promise there will be tons more advice and tips for poop in later chapters, but at this point, don't give up. You might feel that your little one just isn't ready yet, but it's still only day 2! Be consistent and keep experimenting with different activities and rewards until you find a sweet spot.

I haven't mentioned screen time yet because I personally did not want to encourage it at that point, but a tablet with an interactive potty game or short potty videos is definitely worth a try.

END OF DAY REVIEW

Nighttime training is another aspect that we aren't going to go into too much detail about just yet because the focus of the three days is to master daytime training. The standard rule applies, though, which is to be consistent. If you've stopped using diapers, try not to go back now to avoid any confusion. Also, try to reduce the amount your child drinks before bed. Give him his last big drink at least an hour before bedtime so they will have a better chance of peeing before bed.

From my own experience and talking to other parents, there are two common feelings. Pride and joy as your little one makes progress, or utter despair as you open the next pack of disinfectant wipes. Our brains are wired to remember the negative over the positive, so take a moment to process the day genuinely. Was it as bad as you think? Again, what can you do differently to make the potty training easier?

If there is absolutely no sign of progress, this is the time to consider changing something about the routine. I remember someone telling me that the potty should never leave the bathroom and they were horrified at the thought of me having it in the living room or even in the garden. Having the potty somewhere more visible helps as a reminder for your son. You may find that something as simple as moving will encourage him to go without you needing to remind him. The most important thing is that your child feels comfortable going to the potty, even if it's not in the bathroom just yet.

At this point, I also recommend giving yourself a reward! It might be a long soak in the bath (without a potty song playing on repeat in your head), ordering takeout, or watching your favorite series. You are teaching your son essential skills, and although they haven't mastered them yet, you have done well!

This personal reward is a great way to wrap up day 2 and get you back in the right place to start the final stretch. Day 3, here we come.

CHAPTER FIVE. DAY 3: MASTERY AND INDEPENDENCE

If your emotions are mixed as you begin the final day, don't worry. You are allowed to feel all that you are feeling, and it's best to take the time to work through these while your son isn't around. So once again, pour yourself that much-deserved morning coffee!

MORNING BOOST

It's the third and final day of intense training and the process will be very similar to days 1 and 2. Take your few extra moments in the morning to review what is working and areas for improvement. Consider these questions:

- Have I spotted patterns that help recognize when my son needs to use the potty?
- Does my son show signs that he needs to go?
- Is my son happy sitting on the potty and spending enough time there?

- Are we celebrating his successes enough?
- Are there ways we could encourage more motivation?
- Is my son ready to be a little more independent in the process?
- Does he feel ashamed or embarrassed when accidents happen?
- Are my expectations realistic?

The final question is a crucial one. While their routine is still stable and you are keeping a watchful eye on them, for many, day 3 can see some impressive advancement, but this doesn't mean there won't be the odd accident today and beyond.

Some parents put too much mental pressure on this day and assume this is the day when everything goes right, but when this isn't the case, they feel disappointed. Your son is way more emotionally smart than you may think, and he will pick up on the slightest hint of disappointment from you. Day 3 doesn't have to be perfect. There just has to be progress.

Please take a moment to celebrate this day as the last day of the intense training, but there is no need to tell your son that this is day 3 or the last day as this could cause them to feel pressure and high expectations.

That being said, when your son wakes up on day 3, it's time for fun and celebrations to remind them of what a good job they have done so far. If you haven't been out of the house yet, this is definitely a day to treat them to time in the park and even a sweet treat!

ADDRESSING RESISTANCE

When we talk about resistance, it's not related to behavioral problems. We will cover this later on. Resistance is when a child doesn't seem to want to use the potty, even if they know their bodies and the signs. It's often seen in shy children, but that's not to say even the most outgoing and eager-to-please child won't show some resistance at some point.

Resistance can occur for various reasons. We must remember that they are still toddlers, and potty training can feel like they are being rushed to grow up too quickly. It can be extremely frustrating for a parent when their son uses the potty or toilet at daycare but then resists at home, and it's only natural that parents feel like they are doing something wrong.

Day 3 could be the day you notice resistance, which goes back to the pressure, even subconscious pressure to have complete success. Your son may end up sitting on the potty for fear of not upsetting you, but no child can be forced to pee or poop. The pressure might encourage them to rebel as these delightful little people know how to do so well. All of a sudden, a power struggle develops, and it can feel like a standoff with a potty in between!

Your son needs to feel like they are using the potty for them and not because it's something that you need in order to be happy. The authoritative parent works in many situations, like when to eat their veggies or what to wear, but when it's something they have so much control over—when to hold in pee and poop and when not to—they need to feel like they are in control.

Once you have established that they aren't scared of the potty and you are confident that they are happy with their potty choice (again, on day 3, you may need to switch from a toilet to a potty or vice versa), then it's time to take some of that pressure off them. And the first place to start is with a heartfelt apology. By recognizing your mistake and allowing us to make them as parents, you might find that this is enough to take the weight off them.

As resistance is so closely related to control, day 3 may also be a good day to offer them some control in other areas. Giving children the opportunity to make choices gives them essential practice to make good choices when they are older. For toddlers, offering them the choice between what they can have for a snack is more empowering than giving them something they refuse to eat.

The golden rule for offering choices that give children control is to make sure the options give them all the control, as any other approach will backfire. It's common for parents to ask children questions hoping for a particular answer. For instance, during bathtime, you might ask, "Do you want a bath now?" When your child says no, you then have to force the issue and your child is left wondering why you bothered to ask. When giving a choice, make sure that either option the child chooses is a positive outcome for both of you.

When talking to your son about the potty, whether he is sitting on it or you are seeing the signs, make sure you have eye contact with him, which could mean getting down to their level. Eye contact increases attention and trust and can reduce anxiety. It also draws their attention to your facial expressions and that warm, encouraging smile.

Finally, if you are concerned about resistance on this day, ask for help from another adult or even an older sibling. Your son might be picking up on your stress, fueling the power struggle. As soon as someone else lends a hand in the potty-training process, you may find they are still eager to please the other person but there is less resistance.

Anna and Paul's son was a good communicator and used potty language to indicate he wanted to go. He had chosen his potty and was happy sitting on it, but there were only accidents on days 1 and 2. Nobody had been out of the house and both parents were due back at work the following day. Nevertheless, their tone remained positive, and there were plenty of smiles and reassuring words… perhaps a little too over the top!

On day 3, they called for reinforcements and Paul's sister came over. His sister knew they were doing the 3-day potty training method and knew there had been no progress, but after potty training her own three boys, she knew it would happen! When she arrived, she asked Anna and Paul's son if he wanted to go out for a dinosaur ice cream, which was too much for the little boy to refuse. She said, "I need a safety pee before we go. Can you come with me?" and he took her hand, and off they went.

In the bathroom, she made tons of fuss over the cool potty and asked if he would like to try and have a safety pee before going for the dinosaur ice cream, a clever moment of reinforcement. And that was the end of his resistance. Everyone did the potty dance, a big sticker was put on the chart, and Anna and Paul had discovered that for their son, "safety pee" were the magic words.

MOVING TO SELF-INITIATION

Imagine on day 3 that all pee and poop are going in the potty! This is what success must look like and there is good reason to celebrate.

But if you are still reminding them, taking them, pulling down their pants, wiping, pulling up their pants, and so on, there is still a long way to go.

As parents, we have to be careful not to let the fear of accidents stop our sons from gaining independence.

You have dedicated these three days to every step and helping them develop their new skills, but they need the chance to put all of these skills into action.

If you don't want to take any steps back or upset your child's confidence, you need to let them master the whole process because you can't be there every time.

Encouraging potty independence goes back to encouraging dependence through choices in other areas of their lives. At the end of the day, it's more important that your son gets to pick his clothes and get excited to put them on than go out wearing matching clothes.

There are some wonderful books for toddlers that encourage independence. Some of my favorites include:

- ***I Can Do It Myself*** *by Stephen Krensky*
- ***All by Myself*** *by Mercer Mayer*
- ***My Magical Choices*** *by Becky Cummings*

PULLING PANTS DOWN— DOES THAT EVEN MAKE SENSE?

While so much of the focus is on getting that pee and poop in the potty, one particular skill is overlooked, and that is how to teach your toddler to pull his pants and underwear up and down! So many accidents happen simply because they are trying to wriggle out of their pants.

Not only do we not teach them this fundamental part but have you ever considered the vocabulary we use? If you have ever paused to think about whether to push or pull a door, imagine how your little one feels when you tell them to "pull" their pants down. Technically, they are pushing! So, start by clarifying that we push pants down and then pull them up!

Another trick specific to boys is that they need to learn how to push their pants down to their ankles to prevent misfires and accidentally wetting clothes while aiming for the toilet or when they make that transition.

It's common for underwear and pants to come down at the same time, and for now, that's fine as it saves time. However, try to encourage them to pull them up separately to save them from getting in a twist and your son inevitably getting frustrated.

Don't wait for your child to start the potty training to master pushing his pants down and pulling them up again. As soon as you see the sign of needing to go or he feels the urge to go, they should be able to get them down. Zips and buttons are out at this stage but give your son plenty of opportunities to practice putting underwear and pants on and taking them off again. Even consider having pants-tasting parties where they have multiple pairs they can choose from.

When your son can manage a few potty trips where he can complete the steps by himself, you know he has mastered the process, at least for peeing at this stage. An excellent sign is that he will call you when he has finished. As for the sake of cleaning and hygiene, you will need to at least empty the potty and remind him to wash his hands. This is the moment when you don't need to keep such a close eye on your son's every move!

TOP TIPS FOR HANDLING NAP TIMES

Nap times might have gone smoothly and progressed at the same or similar rate as daytime training. Consistency will always be the key. As mentioned before, if you have had a ceremony to ditch the diapers, don't confuse your child by putting a diaper on for naps. Similarly, if you are going bottomless, don't confuse him by putting training pants on for his nap.

Some children may hold on to pee and poop until they have a diaper or training pants on. This will be discussed in detail further on, so keep this in mind. If there has been no pee or poop for a few hours, the moment you put something on them for a nap is the moment they release it!

Your daily observations should have given you plenty of opportunities to notice patterns. In particular, you will have noticed how often they need to pee and how much time passes between a drink (the size of the drink) and pee. It's possible that they also have a preferred time for poop. All of this will help with the timing of naps and staying dry.

The length of a nap is also influential. Most 2-year-olds have one nap a day, but that could be anywhere from one hour to three hours. If you notice your son pees every couple of hours, longer naps could be more problematic. The average 2-year-old needs 13 to 14 hours of sleep. This is an ideal time to start reducing nap times and extending the number of hours they sleep during the night. If a longer nap is pushing bedtime too late, this is the perfect moment to wake them up from their nap and reduce the risk of wetting the bed.

If your toddler has been used to taking a bottle to bed (mine did until he was four!) this is also the time to start weaning them off this habit. A nice way to do that is to have a special "big boy" cup and have some warm milk around an hour before naptime, though this will depend on your observations.

Have them go to the potty or toilet before their nap but avoid saying things like, "You don't want to wet the bed." If accidents happen during nap time, you want to ensure they don't feel more guilt, shame, or embarrassment than they already feel. Instead, take the potty to their room and have it nearby. Remind them that they should call you or whoever will be around if they need to go.

Don't be surprised if nap time takes a little longer to master, especially if they are still sleeping longer. The most important thing to celebrate as you reach the end of day 3 is that the most intense potty training is complete, you are saving money on diapers, and day by day…even hour by hour, there is less cleaning up to do! At this point, the journey is just beginning as we move on to success, which is here to stay!

CHAPTER SIX. POST-3-DAY MAINTENANCE

An assumption some parents and caregivers make is that after three days, their child will be fully potty trained and there will be no more accidents. These are unrealistic expectations for a little person who needs time to develop their newly learned skills. This chapter will cover how to keep working toward potty independence.

MAINTAINING THE MOMENTUM

The hardest part might be over but that doesn't mean your work as master potty trainer is behind you. There may well be some accidents on day 4 and onwards, and this can be greatly reduced by sticking to the routine and reminding your son about using the potty.

By this time, your toddler should be in underwear but don't get carried away with fiddly buttons or zips on their pants just yet. Life will return to normality, which means going to work, leaving the house, and trusting others to continue the progress.

This is most important if your toddler is in daycare. The daycare provider should be over the moon that your son is not in diapers because naturally, it's fewer diapers to change, but you don't want your son's confidence to get knocked by accidents that could have been prevented with stronger communication between you and the daycare center.

Fortunately, multiple ways exist to contact the center, whether by email, an education-based app, or even a short note. You may think a conversation is the best way to communicate, but bear in mind that they are particularly busy at the moment parents drop their children off and pick them up. Written communication is best but let them know you have sent a mail or left a note. Give them as much information as you can so that they have the ability to maintain the rhythm. It's helpful to let them know the vocabulary you use and if you have noticed any particular patterns.

Another thing that should be discussed is the rewards, but this could be a little trickier. From the caregivers' perspective, having a different reward system for each child is a challenge. It's hard to imagine any caregiver not rewarding toddlers for successful potty trips but it's not far if one child has a sticker system and the next doesn't. However, at this point, you still need to keep up with your rewards for a couple more weeks to keep reinforcing the progress.

I have always found it useful to get up a little earlier after the 3-day potty training weekend. There is no guarantee that they will wake up straight away and need to pee or poop. Getting everyone out of the door in the mornings can be stressful as it is without the additional time you might need for additional potty tries.

At this point, having a disposable waterproof sheet in their car seat is also handy, and don't forget those spare clothes. Accidents in the car can be particularly frustrating, especially if you are pressed for time. While you might feel like your toddler kept that pee in just for the car, they truly didn't do it out of spite.

ADDRESSING COMMON POST-3-DAY CHALLENGES

The most common problem parents and caregivers can have is regression. Regression is a setback in the potty-training process. After some success, you might notice that your son goes back to having accidents and not just the odd one here and there, which is expected as they continue to master their skills. They also may not want to use the potty or toilet or even ask to return to using diapers. While this can be baffling for parents, it's perfectly normal.

The causes for regression can be grouped into two main reasons: a change in routine or health reasons. Common changes to a routine that may lead to regression include:

- A new baby in the house
- Moving to a new house
- A divorce or separation
- A change in work schedule for the parents
- A new babysitter
- Starting daycare

- A change of teacher
- Illness in the family
- A recent death in the family

Imagine things that you do automatically, like the laundry or cleaning. When you are stressed or have a lot on your mind, these things might not get done. Though they are only toddlers, they are still susceptible to stress, especially anything traumatic.

Without causing any panic, if regression does occur, you should first book an appointment with your doctor or pediatrician in case of a medical problem. Type 1 diabetes may cause children to pee more frequently. Things like constipation and urinary tract infections (although more common in girls) could be causing immense pain and fear of going to the toilet. Symptoms of a urinary tract infection can include fever, loss of appetite, tiredness, irritability, stomachache, vomiting, or diarrhea. If you see any of these symptoms along with regression, seek medical help.

There are two other reasons regression may occur with your son. It's possible that at this point, you aren't with them every time they go to the bathroom, or at least not there the entire time. Something could occur at this time that causes them to develop a fear of the potty or the toilet. It could be something as simple as slipping or almost falling in.

You will also need to consider the fact they might still need to be ready. In the beginning, boys are more willing to please adults and are highly motivated by rewards. However, as time passes, this willingness to please can fade and the rewards are no longer as enticing, leading to regression. This is why it's even more crucial that potty training is child-led and not something that has to be done to prevent parents from getting angry.

To deal with regression, follow these steps:

1. Identify the cause of regression

Sit down with them and have a reassuring conversation. Make sure you have timed it right when they aren't hungry, tired, or distracted. Ask them if there are any problems or if anything is upsetting or scaring them at the moment.

Give them time to respond and listen carefully to their response. There might be an underlying reason for their stress, and they don't have the means to communicate the issue.

You may also want to ask more specific questions if they don't have the verbal skills to communicate fully. Watch their facial expressions for more information.

If you are worried about them being in pain, ask them to point to where it hurts or use a toy and ask them if they can point to where it hurts on the toy.

2. Visit the doctor

It is always better to be safe than sorry. Doctors will be able to rule out any medical condition and may even be able to help identify psychological problems caused by stress.

From my own experience, ruling out medical issues provided much-needed reassurance, which helped with my stress levels!

3. Work on reducing stressors

Changes to a routine are hard to avoid but it would be a good idea to spend some quality time with your son to remind them of the constants in life. If it's a new sibling, ensure you do activities they love when the baby is napping. Offer them control in a new home by letting them choose how to decorate their room. For more traumatic stressors, it might be worth looking into professional help, especially play therapy, to help them process what they are going through, as it might be affecting them on a deeper level and regression is only part of the issue.

4. Go back to basics

It's likely that what worked in the beginning will work again. If you have stopped the rewards, get the sticker chart back out again. Go back to gentle reminders to use the potty and double-check that their clothes are easy to push down. Be honest with yourself; it might be that you have become less enthusiastic about the success, and it's time to break out of the potty-training dance again. If they don't seem motivated by the original reward system, treat them to a new potty toy or book or allow some screen time to encourage them to sit on the toilet until they are finished.

5. Consider moving the potty

If you are concerned that they have developed a fear of the potty, consider moving it from the bathroom for a while. If it's the sound of the flush that is terrifying them all of a sudden, validate their feelings and let them know that you won't flush the toilet until they have left the bathroom. If they have been using a toilet seat and you are worried that this is causing their fear, it might be worth switching to a potty instead. The additional benefit of moving the potty is that you might be closer to helping them with pants or underwear until they get back into the swing of things.

6. Consider training pants

If your son wants his diapers back, it may be helpful to switch to training pants. The accidents could cause them to feel embarrassed and having training pants may give them more confidence. It will also make your life easier when dealing with accidents. At this point, you need to keep calm no matter what because additional shame could make regression last longer.

It's likely that they will return to just the odd accident within a few days rather than regression. However, in some cases, regression can last a few weeks. If regression lasts more than a month, it might be best to put a hold on potty training because your son could be trying to tell you that he isn't ready yet. If so, don't treat the potty training as a failure. With kind and reassuring words, let them know they can try again later. A month or two doesn't seem like a lot to you, but it's a lot when you consider how fast your son's skills are developing in all areas.

NIGHTTIME INDEPENDENCE

The big question on parents' minds will be when it's okay to start nighttime potty training, and that isn't an easy question to answer. There is no perfect one-age-fits-all because it will depend on their development. Regardless of age, it's worth remembering that a child's physiological development isn't complete until around the age of six, so bedwetting may continue until five or six years old, which would be normal. By this age, the bladder is mature and capable of sending the brain signals to wake up for the toilet.

Generally, you don't want to start nighttime training until they have mastered potty use during the day and you are more or less accident-free. The only reason for this is that you want the daytime training to be full of positive experiences for them and waking up with a wet bed is a bad start to the day. A perfect sign to start the nighttime training is that they generally wake up with a dry diaper/training pants in the morning.

You should already be in the habit of encouraging a potty trip last thing at night and first thing in the morning. To begin training at night, you should limit the amount they drink an hour before bedtime. This may require adjusting the bedtime routine slightly. For example, you may want to offer them a glass of milk, then a bath, pajamas, and a story before bed so there is enough time for the bladder to fill up.

Preparation will make nighttime training easier. Have a potty in their room and a set of supplies in case of an accident. It's wise to keep baby wipes, a spare set of training pants and pajamas, and clean sheets. Having all this in one place will make the change smooth, and both of you will get back to sleep sooner.

Your son must know it's okay to wake you up at night if he needs you. This can be done with the final hug and kiss goodnight in bed. For some, accidents at night may be few and far between but if your child is upset by the number of accidents they have, you can talk to them about why bedwetting happens and that their body isn't quite ready yet, but it will happen. You can also share stories of others who wet the bed when they were younger as a comforting example that this won't last forever.

Each time your son wakes up with a dry bed, it's time to break out the celebrations again. Rewards can include stickers, and after collecting a certain number of stickers, there could be a bigger prize, especially something related to his bed. To give him more independence, you can give him a choice of what he wants for breakfast or what to wear that day.

Regression is something that will probably happen to most toddlers at some point, so you shouldn't worry too much. But what about other hurdles, like when your son refuses to tell you when they want to go or their bathroom behavior is far from what you hoped for? Each child is unique, and the next chapter covers those special scenarios you might encounter, leaving you baffled!

CHAPTER SEVEN. SPECIAL SCENARIOS AND SOLUTIONS

Potty training troubleshooting? Various circumstances can cause parents to wonder what they are doing wrong, from a lack of motivation to trying emotional outbursts and horrendous behavior. Sometimes, all we need is a new perspective to get to the bottom of these situations.

DEALING WITH POTTY FEAR

The first question to ask yourself is whether it's the bathroom or the potty. Moving the potty to a different location will help identify the underlying problem. If it's the bathroom, the next step is to change the environment to make it more inviting for your little one. They might need extra toys or distractions. If this isn't enough to overcome the fear, it's best to use gradual exposure.

Let's imagine each step of going to the potty in detail:

- Entering the bathroom

- Approaching the potty
- Pushing down pants and underwear
- Sitting on the potty
- Peeing or pooping
- Wiping
- Pulling pants and underwear up
- Flushing
- Washing hands

To use gradual exposure, you would first only take your son to the bathroom door. Hug them, show them with love, and let them know that everything is okay. Walk away and then return to the bathroom door. Keep repeating this until your son shows no sign of fear. The next step is to take them to the potty without any expectations except to help them get there. You may notice the same signs of fear as before when they got to the bathroom door, but more love and hugs will help them overcome their fears. It's essential that you only move on to the next stage once your little one is entirely comfortable. Always keep in mind that they need to be in control, and they shouldn't be overcoming their fears to make you happy.

YOUR SON JUST WON'T TELL YOU

There are several ways to overcome a communication barrier. Still, bear in mind that the main goal is to get any amount of pee or poop in the potty. If you notice signs of them needing to go and there is no fear of the potty, you might need to pick them straight up, push their clothes down, and put them on the potty so that you can celebrate the achievement.

If you can see they are in mid-accident, don't wait for them to finish. I know it's messy, but they need to discover the connection between feeling the discomfort of their accident and the potty.

Regarding language, remember the importance of consistency when using words that correlate with the steps going to the toilet. Better yet, lead by example. Say things like, "I had a big drink, and now I need to pee in the bathroom." Support this with typical actions like holding your crotch or doing a bit of a wiggle. If you have spotted their signs of needing to go, mimic them.

In the final chapter, you will discover nonverbal cue cards that can help those who aren't using any vocabulary, but another simple solution is to have a potty pal! In the bathroom, you can keep their special toy or book, and in addition, get into the habit of taking their potty pal to the bathroom with them and also every time you go. They will begin to associate the potty pal with signs of needing to go. When you see them looking for, asking for, or picking up their potty pal, you know it's time to get them to that potty.

SCREAMING AND PROTESTING

Screaming, protesting, temper tantrums, intentionally peeing or pooping on the floor, and even hitting are all considered bad behavior. Still, in most cases, our own bias of good and bad behavior leads us to miss the point. Their behavior is often their attempt to communicate something to us, and as a parent, it's our job to uncover the information they are trying to tell us.

Some causes for acting out can include:

- Fear or anxiety
- Health issues like constipation
- Not understanding the steps properly
- Difficulty breaking down the steps
- Frustration from not being able to communicate with you
- Boundary pushing, which is part of their development
- They aren't ready for potty training

Before attempting to overcome behavioral issues, you need to find the cause. Ask yourself the following questions:

- What is your son getting from this behavior?
- What are they not getting from this behavior?
- What makes the behavior continue or escalate?
- What stops the behavior?
- What happens leading up to your son's behavior?

Identifying the problem can help you adjust the process, and remember that if you think it's medical, the first thing to do is see a doctor.

Parenting is full of blessings but it's also hard, and when it comes to aggressive behavior, it takes everything in us to respond and not react. When we react, we are basing our actions on emotions, and more often, this will be our anger and frustration. We take the emotion, process it, and respond appropriately when we respond. A couple of deep breaths can make all the difference in your behavior and the outcome. It also gives you just enough time to think about how your son might be feeling at that moment.

To handle behavior problems that aren't related to medical issues or readiness, it's important to go back to the basics and break down the process into simpler steps for them to grasp. This includes reducing verbal cues and keeping instructions easier for them.

Always go back to the step that they have mastered. If they get into the bathroom without any problems but the behavior starts when they try to push their pants down, go back to the previous stage. When they are showing signs of needing to potty, go to the bathroom together and push their pants down, then help them push them down. Eventually, they will be able to do the same without outbursts. You might need to repeat the patience for each step!

REWARDS DON'T MOTIVATE

One of the biggest mistakes we can make is to go too big and too bold with the first set of rewards, giving us no backup plan. Rewarding toddlers with luxurious gifts takes the focus away from mastering their skills. You also may find yourself in a position where you find it difficult to find the appropriate motivation for other skills that they will have to develop.

The first reward should always be praise, love, affection, and excitement. Other non-material options could be sending a message to the other parent, another special adult, or a phone call (only if you know the other person will respond with the necessary excitement).

For material rewards, keep the items small, like stickers or crayons, and make sure they are in their line of sight. Don't give it to them until there has been some success. If there is no pee or poop, let them know that it's okay, the reward will still be there for the next time. Whatever reward you choose, it has to be immediate! Toddlers can't make the connection between behavior and reward, so if it isn't immediate, they won't relate pee or poop in the potty with their reward.

If you feel you have gone a little over the top with your original rewards, don't be too hard on yourself; we have all been there! If your son isn't motivated by typical rewards, it's time to increase the fun level in the process.

First of all, is your son's potty or toilet seat the best in the house? Is it a place that makes them happy and smile? If not, it's time to decorate it. If the stickers are almost working but not on a chart, you could see if they are more excited by decorating the potty with a sticker every time they successfully use it to cover the entire outside of it.

If your son is sitting, try putting a few drops of blue food coloring in the potty or toilet. They will be amazed to see how pee turns the toilet water green. You might have to do this first to show them. If they are standing, make it more fun by adding a few Cheerios or similar cereals as target practice. If they have a potty pal, let them play the role of parent and teach their pal the steps because some children will be more motivated by responsibility than material rewards.

REFUSING TO BE WITHOUT PULL-UPS

This is another area where forcing the issue may do more harm than good. Consider why your son refuses to be without pull-ups. The most logical explanation is that he is embarrassed or ashamed because of his accidents and an empathetic parent can see how this would deeply affect their son.

Give them time to develop their skills and confidence. After a week or so, you can suggest big boy underwear, and if they aren't willing, try again in another week or so. Keep up the praise for all their dry days and keep showing them different underwear to see if there is one in particular that gets them excited. The point will come where they make the decision to ditch the pull-ups, but they need to feel ready for this and not pressured.

HOLDING IN PEE AND POOP

To overcome holding in pee or poop, you first need to eliminate the possible reasons for this, starting with anxiety or fear of the potty or bathroom, which again, might be as simple as just moving the potty, removing the source of fear, or not flushing when they are in the bathroom.

If your son is sitting on the toilet seat and is wobbling all over the place, there is going to be a fear of slipping or falling. Instead of expressing this fear, they might be holding their pee or poop. Switching to a potty can remove this fear.

You may need to find ways to make your son more relaxed, such as playing music, singing songs together, or dimming the lights.

This may sound contradictory but holding in pee and poop may also be a sign of your toddler not being ready. They have the skill to recognize a full bladder and even hold it, but there is a physiological reason for them not to want to use the potty or toilet. For the sake of their health, please don't force it. Holding in poop is a little more complex, and we will cover this in more detail in the following chapters.

Typically, children need to pee every two to three hours. If you notice it has been six hours, you should seek medical advice. If it has been over 12 hours and they are sleepy or hard to wake up, you should seek urgent help.

POTTY TRAINING THE STRONG-WILLED CHILD

The strong-willed little boy knows what he wants and when he wants it. He likes being independent, and if he doesn't want to do something, he simply won't. The decision to potty train will have to come from them, which can be annoying if you hope to have the intense training done by a specific time.

The best way to encourage him to start using the potty is to plan ahead with books, stories, positive examples of older siblings, and videos. Give them the choice of potty and underwear, but have them ready in the bathroom rather than jumping straight into using them. Set up a new system where older siblings or parents get rewards every time they go to the bathroom. Let them see that there is something exciting they could be missing out on, but don't exclude them or remind them they aren't "big" enough to join in. Let them know that the potty or toilet seat is ready for them whenever they want to try.

Allowing strong-willed children to have some control is essential, and this should also begin before potty training. Try to offer up to two choices; each choice has to be something you are happy with. What is probably even more crucial is that all adults are on the same page when it comes to giving options to make sure the control remains "controlled." If an adult offers two choices but gives in to a third option the toddler has suggested, the adult relinquishes control, undermining their own efforts.

Being strong-willed isn't something you want to discourage. It makes parenting a toddler harder, but in years to come when they stand up for what they believe is correct, you will admire this amazing quality!

POTTY TRAINING TWO AT ONCE

It may feel like you are about to have double the work but it doesn't necessarily mean double the pain. Potty training two children at once can provide a small benefit in motivating each other and providing each other with positive examples.

You already know that your children have entirely different personalities and that isn't going to change during potty training. The biggest mistake would be to assume they will both be ready at the same time or compare them to each other. That being said, you should treat them both equally and fairly, especially when it comes to praise and encouragement.

The 3-day method is the same whether it's one child or two, but of course, it will be more intense for you, and it does mean watching both of them like hawks. It's wise to see if there is another adult who can be around, at least for some time, to help you on day 1 or possibly day 2. This will make noticing patterns and signs easier. If need be, write the times of pees and poops because as much as we want to tell ourselves, we will remember after a potty dance or an accident the times are not the first thing that comes to mind. Sticking to a strict routine will help!

You will need double of everything. There is nothing special about a potty if you have to share it with your sibling, and if they both need to go at the same time, it's not fair that one has to wait. They also deserve to pick out their own new underwear, special potty toys or books, and their own rewards. Each child also has to understand that their potty-training equipment is special to them and they can't take their sibling's things.

Regarding the rewards, buy double in case. If you can see that one child is motivated by their sibling's rewards, you can't take their rewards away, but you can have a spare. You can also use these opportunities to encourage sharing. You will want to start by taking them both to use the potty at the same time so you can encourage sharing or swapping books each potty time. If there is resistance, don't force it.

Unless you have any particular reason for starting in pull-ups, training pants, or underwear, you may want to strongly consider going bottomless for at least the first day, only because of the additional laundry.

WHEN TO STOP THE REWARDS

First of all, you need to make sure that accidents are infrequent and that they are using the potty successfully for at least days at a time. It's still not practical to expect perfection. This can take a week or two and, in some cases, longer.

There are several ways to stop rewards. One way is to go cold turkey and stop them all at once, but personally, I have never had the heart for this. Such a shock to their routine could cause regression and all of a sudden, you are back to square one.

A second option is only to give rewards when they ask for one; eventually, they will forget about the rewards. You can see that this approach will depend on your son's personality. If you notice any increase in accidents, it might be necessary to restart the reward system after each success.

My personal favorite was to gradually reduce the rewards, replacing smaller ones with something larger at the end of the day and something non-material. I used a choice of dinner at the end of each day without pee accidents but kept up the stickers for every successful poop. Then we went down to choosing a movie at the end of every accident-free week (pee and poop). Eventually, this went down to people taking turns choosing a movie when the connection between clean weeks and choosing movies had disappeared.

POTTY TRAINING OUT AND ABOUT

Mastering potty training out of the home can be incorporated into the 3-day plan if things are going well and you both feel positive; however, I would still recommend day 1 at home and day 2 going out if you have to. It goes without saying at this point that the first thing is to get into the routine of trying to go to the toilet before leaving the house and for your first few trips to be short ones. Before leaving, ensure you have wipes and spare clothes, such as two or three sets, as it's better safe than sorry.

It's a case of trusting your gut here! In some cases, having the potty in one place is the ideal solution to fit in with the routine. On the other hand, moving the potty to different rooms allows your son to adjust to peeing or pooping in different environments, reducing the stress of using public toilets. Don't force this during the 3-day training. The priority is always success and celebrations in the home. You may feel it's best to wait a few more days before moving the potty, and of course, if they are using the toilet, you won't have this flexibility unless you buy a potty for this reason. Again, it's down to understanding your son because this may also confuse them.

When possible, let your son choose the first few places they want to visit when leaving home. If you know you have to go out at a certain time to a particular place, try to have a short outing before that gives them a choice. The reason for this is that if they are happy about where they are, they will feel less worried or anxious, which means a greater chance of them communicating with you, and you can reduce the risk of them holding it in.

Consider reducing the fluid intake for an hour before going out. Nevertheless, we can't border on being cruel. It's more of only giving them fluids when they ask for a drink rather than encouraging drinking for a successful potty trip.

Many facilities now have special "mini" toilets for toddlers and children. If you are in an area where you know there are these toilets, ask them if they want to go or, better yet, go yourself and see if this encourages them to use the mini toilet.

Travel Potty Seats

As it's not always possible to find a mini toilet, the next best thing is a travel potty seat. When I first heard of this, I imagined looking like a crazy mom walking around with half a toilet seat hanging out of my bag, but fortunately, someone came up with folding travel potty seats. Here are some great and affordable examples:

- **Jool** Baby Folding Travel Potty Seat
- **Maliton** Portable Foldable Travel Seat for Toddler & Kid
- **Gimars** Upgraded Non-Slip Silicone Pads Folding Portable Travel Seat

Portable Potty Chair

An alternative to a foldable potty seat is a foldable potty because this gives you more flexibility when public toilets aren't available. If your child also shows signs of fear of public toilets, a foldable potty is ideal to get them confident at home with the same potty before venturing out.

Toilet Seat Covers (Disposable)

Finally, another simple option is to use toilet seat covers. They don't provide the same stability as a portable toilet seat, but if this isn't a problem for your son, having a cover might create a sense of familiarity because they can be used at home for a practice run before going out.

For me, the biggest learning curve, after patience and not reacting, was trying to understand why the behavior and potential challenges to potty training were occurring. From here, I could work backward to find the solution. I also know that with a million other things going on, it's not always as simple just to sit and think about why your son seems to love driving you mad by peeing on the floor! Take advantage of the quiet mornings, naps, and evenings when they are asleep. There are other things that need to be done but reflection will save you time and emotional strain!

The following chapter continues with potential challenges from a different perspective. Toddlers with learning and physical disabilities will need more support from their parents without causing more stress!

CHAPTER EIGHT. ADDRESSING ADDITIONAL NEEDS

Additional needs may bring about extra challenges, but that's not to say that it's impossible, nor do you need to wait longer to start. The first thing is to make sure you talk to your doctor so that your son has all the proper support and resources to gain confidence using the potty. Let's begin with the unique challenges children with additional needs may face.

UNIQUE CHALLENGES

The process of going to the bathroom is something that adults rarely think about, but in total, it requires more than 40 cognitive and physical skills. That's a lot for any little person to process, let alone a child with additional needs. Nevertheless, with the right considerations and adaptations, potty training in three days is still achievable. There is no evidence to support waiting until children with additional needs are older to potty train. In fact, waiting longer may make it harder to introduce a new place for them to pee and poop.

Like any other child, it's about knowing when they are ready. Aside from readiness signs we have covered, your son should be able to follow one or two simple instructions such as "Pick up the teddy and put him in the basket." Don't forget that it's possible your child won't show signs of readiness.

Some parents don't wait for signs of readiness because their child can't express their feelings or communicate. Instead, they will check the diaper every hour or so to get a better idea of their child's toilet habits. Once they have a better idea, they take the diaper off and put them on the potty. The goal is still the same—any amount of pee or poop is progress and begins the connection between needing to pee or poop and the potty.

One of the biggest challenges for parents can be the communication barrier. Parents will need to explore different nonverbal cues, whether visual cards or sign language. And this is essential to master before starting potty training so the risk of holding in pee and poop is prevented.

Children with learning delays and disorders may find it difficult to remember each step, so it's even more important to break them down and master one before moving on to the next. Visual cues should be used, and if you are using visual cues as part of their daily routine, it's good to add an image of the potty or toilet first thing in the morning, before daycare, before/after meals, and before bed.

Another unique challenge you might face is if your child suffers from sensory processing problems, which are often associated with conditions such as autism spectrum disorder (ASD) and attention deficit hyperactivity disorder (ADHD). Extra care and attention will be needed to ensure the environment is perfect for them to feel relaxed.

A child with physical disabilities may struggle with muscle development. It can take longer for them to learn how to control the necessary muscles, and it's normal for them to take longer to master independence with potty training. Depending on the physical disability, specialized toilets or toilet seats might be needed.

Above all, you will need to be extra patient and understanding. You have seen your child struggle as they master other skills, and you know that they get there in the end, but this is a skill that can lead to accidents that bring about all kinds of upsetting feelings for them, which can be more frustrating if they are unable to communicate with you about this. Respect and love your child's individuality, just as you always have!

TAILORED STRATEGIES

The process is going to be the same. First, you are going to introduce the concept of the potty and get everyone excited about choosing their special potty and underwear. Your son likely gets upset when routines are changed, and it's possible that they don't show signs of readiness. For these reasons, it's best to start teaching them the skills they will need before potty training begins as a gradual introduction to new concepts.

The significant difference will be taking the time to ensure your son has fully mastered each step before moving on, and you may need to be there to give extra help. For example, you may need to lower their pants down for them for a while and then encourage them to take over this task by asking them to push their pants down to their ankles. It's possible that they will also need help with wiping for longer.

Social stories are excellent for children with additional needs in all areas of their life and creating your own can be especially useful for your son because it will be more personalized, particularly if they require a different type of toilet.

Whether your child uses a potty or the toilet, you should let them make the choice unless you feel you know which is better. Those children who don't like changes to the routine might prefer to use the toilet straight away. On the other hand, a potty is the perfect height to have their knees higher than their hips and their feet flat on the floor—the best position for going poop! If you are going to use the toilet, have a footstool nearby so they can place their feet on it and be in this ideal position.

Potty and Toilets with More Stability

Here are some ideas that may provide additional stability and reassurance:

- Rabb 1st Potty Training Seat
- Potty Training Seat with Removable Cushion
- Child Commode/Shower Chair

Getting the environment right has to be a priority, especially for children with sensory processing problems. I think this is something tough for adults to understand, and it's time to walk a few steps in their shoes. Imagine the most horrible thing you can think of to touch. For me, it's Scotch-Brite, which is a brand of scouring pads for cleaning. The texture is enough to make me cringe thinking about it. The mere thought of sitting on a toilet seat made of Scotch-Brite makes me never want to go again! Now, imagine a normal light bulb that is so intense it's like you are looking at the sun or a soap that burns your skin upon contact.

It's not just a sensory overstimulation (hypersensitivity) that can impede going to the bathroom. Hyposensitivity is when a person experiences a low level of sensory feedback or none at all. Children may have to move more often, fidget, or flap to experience a sense of movement and they might have trouble with balance, so a toilet with more stability is a must. Typically, we would play some nice, quiet music to help a child relax. A hyposensitive child might be more relaxed with louder music and even brighter lights. This can also be dangerous when washing hands and hot water as they might not sense how hot the water actually is. If you are concerned, getting a special lock for your faucets is a good idea.

To create a sensory-friendly bathroom, consider the following options:

- Choose a light bulb that can be adjusted, even change colors
- Don't put mirrors near windows because it creates a glare

- Have large soft bath mats on hard floors

- Choose a soft-closing toilet seat to prevent loud bangs when they close

- Ensure the equipment they need is nonslip

- Choose scent-free hand soap and avoid strong-smelling cleaning products

Bear in mind that if your child has sensory processing problems, you might also need to adjust your celebrations. Not all children will enjoy a hug, a high-five, or a cheering parent. Don't forget the power of a smile and blowing kisses, even silent clapping.

Motivation can be tricky. You might have noticed that your little one has so much to deal with, and the thought of being a "big boy" doesn't motivate them because they are safer in their existing world without adding to their problems. Again, discovering rewards that motivate can be explored before potty training begins.

As there are so many additional needs and spectrums, we will cover some special considerations.

- **Physical disabilities:** It's best to consult with your doctor and, particularly, an occupational therapist to discuss their unique challenges.

- **Visual disabilities:** Make sure the bathroom is well-ventilated and smells nice, the potty is always in the same place, and there are no obstacles in their path. Talk through the process with them, even let them use their hands to feel your pants around your ankles and on your shoulders so they know you are sitting.

A musical potty can make the process more fun for them. Let them practice pulling off short amounts of toilet paper and have them feel the inside of the potty rim to know where the toilet paper goes.

• **Hearing disabilities:** You will need to introduce more sign language or Makaton gestures if you are using this as a form of communication. Before beginning potty training, use "wet" and "dry" actions with sad and happy facial expressions.

• **Continence problems:** Some conditions won't affect their cognitive abilities but will have an impact on their physical abilities, which can be even more frustrating for them.

If this is the case, it's best to take your son to the potty every hour or so until it becomes a regular habit in their daily routine. After some time, you can just remind them every hour or so.

• **Cerebral palsy:** The main concern will be muscle control and medications that can cause constipation. Plenty of fluids and a high-fiber diet will help. Velcro on clothing can be useful, and you may find it easy for your son to practice removing clothes lying down.

• **Spina bifida and spinal cord injury:** Most children won't be able to detect when they need to go, and without recognizing a full bowel, they are at greater risk of constipation. Your pediatrician and therapist are the best sources of support.

• **Behavioral/cognitive delays and disorders:** Knowing your child's strengths, weaknesses, habits, and interests is key to successful potty training. The early days will be the most important. Day 1 and even day 2 have to be calm and additional patience from you means their frustration won't escalate and set the wrong tone for the rest of the process.

THE IMPORTANCE OF KNOWING YOUR CHILD

Stephine and John have an autistic 3-year-old who is nonverbal. He uses visual cards to point to things he needs and wants. His parents added a potty visual card a few weeks before potty training began and monitored his diapers to record all pees and poops. They knew that he loved to build things, so they had decided a Spidey Lego set would be a great motivator with every trip to the potty building up Spidey.

They were pleased when their son started using the visual cues but couldn't understand why he wouldn't use the potty. He would enter the bathroom and, without sitting on the potty, shake his head and walk out, only to have an accident.

On a different matter, their son also had an issue with food and would only eat yellow (or at least pale) foods. Any other color caused him anxiety. So, rather than pushing him to use the awesome Spidey potty they had bought, they chose a new yellow potty, a yellow sticker chart, yellow baby wipes, even a yellow soap dispenser, and a special yellow towel to dry his hands on. This was enough to reduce his anxiety, and he began to start using the potty.

SEEKING EXPERT HELP

The internet is a double-edged sword when it comes to expert help. While there are so many websites that can offer guidance and advice, it's also a rabbit hole. You will sometimes find conflicting advice, and no website is going to be able to take into consideration your unique child. You may also find yourself researching something only to start imagining symptoms that aren't really a cause for concern, especially when it comes to developmental stages. The best place to start will always be your family doctor, who will then be able to recommend a specialist if necessary, and the sooner, the better. Trust your instincts!

If you want some reassurance from the internet, stick to reputable sources with information that is specific to your child. This could include Autism Speaks, NHS, or ChildCare.

Forums are great for general advice, sharing stories, and finding some much-needed reassurance from parents going through similar issues, but potty training is one part of your child's development, and the appropriate resources and help are needed for each step of their journey!

When I was researching for my own children, I was overwhelmed by the advice for pee, but when it came to the poop, which was honestly my least favorite clean-up, information was limited! Potty training can't ignore one of the two bodily functions, so in the next chapter, it's time to get more familiar with what's going on in these little bowels.

CHAPTER NINE. UNDERSTANDING THE POOP PUZZLE

Since there was so little advice on poop, I was determined to take away all the stigma and silence around poop training. Get comfortable as we begin with a little anatomy lesson and why poop takes more relaxation!

INTRODUCTION TO POOP TRAINING

For some fortunate parents, pee and poop training go hand in hand, but this isn't true for most. At around a year old, children are able to sense when their bowels are full, but they don't have the ability to control the muscles that allow them to hold them in long enough to get to the bathroom.

Let's look at things from a practical point of view. The more you practice a skill, the easier it becomes. Your toddler can pee every couple of hours but may only poop once or twice a day, so they don't have the same opportunities to practice bowel control as they do bladder control.

There is naturally a physiological difference too. There are two sets of muscles involved in going to the toilet, all found within the pelvic floor muscles. Pee and poop are controlled by two muscles called the sphincters. The larger sphincter is around the anus, while the smaller one is around the urethra. We can control the sphincter around the urethra, which is why we can pee and not poop at the same time. To poop, all of the muscles need to be relaxed, which your son may find more challenging.

From a physiological point of view, your son may have seen you pee a million times, but let's face it—we all have limits to our privacy. Though this is totally unintentional, toddlers may already start associating poop differently to pee and feel more shame. This may explain why your son is perfectly happy to pee on the floor in front of you but will go and hide to poop.

For these reasons, it's possible that you will come across some unique challenges when it comes to getting that poop in the potty. They might feel more secure with a diaper on but remember that as long as they are still in a diaper, they will still learn that pooping while standing up is normal.

Some children see poop as a part of their physical self. It can be pretty scary for them to poop in the potty or toilet for fear of losing this "body part." There are potential sensory issues too, especially if water or pee splashes on their bottoms.

It's a myth to think that your son has mastered peeing in the potty and, therefore, poop will follow naturally. Some children will have control of their poop within three days or soon after but don't worry if it takes longer. It's important to manage your expectations so that you aren't putting unnecessary pressure on your son because the last thing you want is for them to start holding poop in or regressing when it comes to peeing.

RECOGNIZING POOP READINESS SIGNS

As mentioned before, typical signs that your little one needs to poop are in the facial expressions, especially signs of strain or possibly pain. They may hold their stomach or bottom and bend over at the waist. You may also hear grunts.

If they use words, they may say "potty" or the same keyword you have used. Don't be surprised if they also say, "no potty." If you have been having success with pee but not so much with the poop, you might want to consider a new visual cue card.

When unraveling the poop puzzle, it helps to talk to your son about what they are feeling when they need to poop. This way, they can link that particular feeling with the need to go. You can say that their bottom feels full or that there is a tickling feeling inside. Talking about these sensations normalizes poop and can remind them that it's all natural and nothing to be ashamed about.

Seeking privacy is a common sign with toddlers. They may go into a different room, particularly the bathroom. They may also hide somewhere, like behind a couch. Also, pay attention to the eye contact they make. Some toddlers may avoid eye contact, whereas others will make intense eye contact with you. Others will stare into space as if daydreaming.

One of the best signs to hope for, and this may occur before the 3-day training begins, but if your son tells you they have pooped or bring a clean diaper for you to change them, they are well on the way to being ready for pooping in the potty. It's always a good idea to start taking the dirty diaper and going to the bathroom with your son so that you can flush the poop away together. This way, they begin to associate poop with the bathroom and the toilet.

While you have more chances to catch a few drops of that pee in the potty, the poop may only happen once or twice a day, and more often than not, the timing is a little more regular. If, after keeping track of their times, you notice that they poop mid-afternoon, it's a good practice to pop them on the potty or toilet at that time of day.

A CHILD'S PERSPECTIVE OF POOP

For a little person, it's surprising how scary the poop process is, and more so when they are using the toilet. There can be a level of insecurity with their legs dangling as they grip onto the sides in fear they are going to fall in. The strange sound of the flush can also be unnerving, making them feel like they're about to be sucked into the abyss. And to top it off, the toilet seat is often cold, adding to the discomfort of the experience.

Fear can also occur after a painful poop, which can cause a child to hold in their poop, which unfortunately just increases the risk of another painful poop. If your son has a diaper rash, pooping is likely to be painful; however, going bottomless during the first day or two can help clear up this rash. Sometimes, illness, a change in diet, dehydration, and even hot weather could make potty training and poop more challenging.

Toddlers can become so engrossed in what they are doing that they don't want to stop using the potty, and this applies to pee and poop. But let's face it, the thought of going through this scary and potentially painful process is rarely more exciting than what they are doing at that moment. And again, though it may seem irrational, from their point of view, pooping in a public toilet while out and about is going to be more terrifying.

CREATING A POSITIVE POOP ENVIRONMENT

I am a big fan of getting down to a toddler's level to understand things better from their point of view. You may feel silly but take a moment to sit on the bathroom floor and imagine how they see things. It can give you a whole new perspective on your son's fears.

Considering the need for relaxed muscles, it's essential that you make the necessary changes to help your son overcome these poop-related fears.

The first potential change could be the toilet. If your son is happy to pee in the potty but not poop, or vice versa, consider making changes. It might feel like you are confusing things or breaking the routine, but it's worth it if it prevents them from holding poop in.

A heated toilet seat is a little extreme but until they gain confidence, it would be nice if the bathroom were warmer to help them feel more comfortable.

Another factor that could affect their bathroom experience is the lighting, especially if it's too bright. Consider a dimmer light or using a lamp instead of a whole light.

Smell is another potential hurdle. I got a special air freshener and let my son choose a scent, and as part of his reward, he was allowed to give the air freshener an extra squirt. It doesn't seem like much, but for him, it made the process more fun and less smelly!

If you think sound is causing a problem, some music can help, especially if it's the sound poop makes in the toilet. And, if the splash annoys them, put some toilet paper in the bowl or potty before they go to prevent any unwanted splashing.

PSYCHOLOGICAL OR PHYSIOLOGICAL?

Most issues with poop are because of fear, anxiety, or distractions. Nevertheless, there could be a few physical reasons for withholding their poop. Some gastrointestinal conditions cause chronic constipation, such as celiac disease, irritable bowel syndrome, and, in some cases, lactose intolerance. Frequent constipation can lead to hard poop getting stuck in the colon, and colonic inertia is when the gastrointestinal system can't efficiently move poop along. Pelvic floor dysfunction or the sphincter muscle around the anus being too tight are possible anatomical problems.

There is no need to panic because the lack of poop in the potty is more often than not psychological. But if you have ruled out any other issue and/or your son is in pain, definitely see a doctor.

BOOKS TO HELP THE POOP PUZZLE

Books are a great way to make poop a normal part of life. You can use these books as part of story time or as their particular book for reading on the potty. Either way, they are a chance to have a little fun with your son!

- ***The Dinosaur That Pooped a Plant!*** *by Tom Fletcher and Dougie Poynter*
- ***Come Out Mr. Poo!*** *by Janelle McGuinness*
- ***"Bloop, Bloop!" Goes the Poop*** *by Temara Moore*

You don't necessarily have to spend money on a book. Don't forget that you can also make your own social story based on your son's unique personality and preferences using photos or even simple stick-figure drawings. In the next chapter, we will discover bonus tips and techniques to help get that poop in the potty.

CHAPTER TEN. SETTING THE STAGE FOR SUCCESSFUL POOP TRAINING

You may have noticed that there is little attention given to poop potty training until there is actually a problem with constipation. Taking the time to get it right from the beginning is the best practice to prevent constipation and, therefore, more problems later down the road!

THE POOP TALK

To help relax your toddler, talking about poop can take the shame away from this natural and necessary bodily process. On one level, there is talking about poop and the potty, but there is a whole other level of conversation that can reassure your little one.

The best thing about children at this age is that their brains are literally powerhouses. They absorb information with little to no effort, mainly because most of their learning is through play and fun. They are curious, and we can use this to our advantage. Have you considered whether your son understands the relationship between food and poop?

I'm not suggesting that you explain to your little one how digestive juices break food molecules down into smaller ones before nutrients are absorbed into the bloodstream. However, toddlers are capable of understanding that when we eat food, the body takes all the yummy vitamins to give us energy and grow strong, and then we pee and poop out what the body doesn't need.

Instead of poop seeming like a part of their body they are losing, young children can understand that poop is what the body doesn't need, and as long as there is more food, there is more poop!

To reinforce the connection between food and poop, I discovered a fun toy called Gotta Go Turdle, a toilet-trained turtle who likes to eat, sing, and of course, poop. Shelbert the turtle comes with a type of sand used for food. After you feed him the sand, his neck wiggles as the "food" moves down his neck. There is a song and a bit of dancing before Shelbert announces, "Uh oh, gotta go," and he poops on the included toilet. The food can be separated from the water in the bowl and reused. But even better, Shelbert repeats what you say, so you can make this a personalized poop-training educational game.

THE POOP ROUTINE

Poop can tell a lot about a person's health, so it's natural to feel like you might be a little obsessed about examining what is going on and what someone considers normal. It goes without saying that diet will have a huge impact on poop, but we will cover this in the next section. Drinking enough water will help ensure poop doesn't become hard and painful to pass. On the other hand, sugary drinks may lead to dehydration.

A child's level of activity can also change the poop routine. Physical activity stimulates the movement of food and digestion, and it flexes different muscles. While toddlers don't have the same problems as adults, they still suffer from stress, which can put pressure on their body functions, especially the digestive system. Stress and different medications disrupt the normal bacteria in the gut, which can have a knock-on effect.

Finally, as babies grow into toddlers, it's common to see fewer poops. What's considered normal can be anywhere from one or two poops a day to one every couple of days. It's more important to track changes to determine what is normal for them.

Check the Bristol Stool Chart

If you are concerned, using a stool tracker to inform your doctor exactly what's happening would be helpful. One of the most common trackers is the Bristol Stool Chart, which can be found via the link on the right.

It's a great idea to try and encourage toddlers to poop at the same time each day, which may sound like an impossible task but it's a good way to regulate their bowel movements and promote healthy poop habits. It also makes it easier to spot any potential irregularities or problems. Gently remind your son to sit on the potty for a poop 20 to

30 minutes after a meal and after a bath. During these times, action in the gut speeds up, increasing the chances of getting that poop in the potty.

A satisfying way to end the poop process routine is to have a goodbye ritual. With all three of my children, we would pour the contents of the poop into the toilet, flush, and give the poop a little wave as we said goodbye. Even now, I rarely ask if they have flushed the toilet but if they said goodbye!

YOUR SON'S DIET

In the next chapter, we will take a closer look at what to do when your son is constipated, but for now, let's focus on what a healthy balanced diet can do for the poop puzzle and routine!

After all, the proper diet isn't only crucial for potty training. It's also essential to ensure they have all the nutrients they need for healthy growth and development. Their diet must give them the energy they need to remain active, supporting regular bowel movements.

Ideally, toddlers should eat five meals daily, three of these main meals and two snacks. The following food types can be broken down into each of the meals. When we say portions, it means the same amount as their clasped fist.

- **Grains and starchy carbohydrates:** Five portions of foods such as cereals, bread, rice, pasta, and potatoes to get enough energy and vitamin B. Whole grains have more nutrients and fiber but can also fill toddlers up more, so add these to the diet gradually.

- **Fruits and vegetables:** Ideally, there will be five portions of fruit and vegetables of different colors. This can be fresh, dried, frozen, or canned if it entices them. Fruit juice is considered one portion but be careful because of the sugar content. Also, juices don't always contain the same fiber as a whole vegetable or piece of fruit.

- **Milk and dairy:** Cheese, yogurt, and milk are ideal to help toddlers get their three servings of this food group. After their second birthday, it's okay to introduce semi-skimmed milk while they are eating a balanced diet. Avoid rice milk until they are five because of the potential arsenic levels.

- **Meats and proteins:** Two portions of proteins are necessary at this age. Protein comes from meat, fish, eggs, beans, pulses, lentils, and nuts. These food types are also high in other nutrients like iron and zinc.

As a fussy eater myself and the mom of a fussy eater, I know it's hard to get this ideal balance. Don't be scared to get creative with foods, especially when introducing something new. It's amazing how much more excited a toddler is to try a new vegetable that is part of a clown face on a pizza topping compared with just having it on a plate.

Don't lose hope if your son doesn't want to try a new food straight away or if, at first, they don't like it. Like me, you might be from the generation of adults who sat there and practically forced you to try something when you were a kid, and this only leads to an unhealthy relationship with food.

Much like potty training, working toward a balanced diet is about positive reinforcement. Forcing the issue leads to a power struggle, whereas giving them a choice to try a new food gives them enough independence to want to try. And if they don't, try again in a couple of days. When they do try something new, let them know how proud you are that they tried it—it doesn't matter if it's only the tiniest of nibbles!

KEEPING TODDLERS HYDRATED

Toddlers sometimes listen to their body's messages, which can be the case when it comes to staying hydrated. Liquids are essential to keep the poop soft and moving through the intestines. Even the slightest dehydration can lead to constipation.

Being extremely thirsty is an obvious sign that your son is dehydrated, as is the color of their pee. It should be a pale yellow. Other signs of more severe dehydration to be aware of are that they are less active than usual or seem lethargic, irritable, or confused. They may have cold hands or feet and their skin could be pale. It's possible that their heart rate increases and they become dizzy. Severe dehydration requires immediate medical attention.

The ideal amount of liquids is around four to six cups of water or milk, likely more in warmer weather. If it's hard to get your son to drink enough fluids, try changing the temperature of the water or infusing water with fruit or herbs.

Another way to help increase their fluid intake is to offer hydrating foods such as watermelon, grapes, and oranges. You can even make smoothies and freeze them for a fun treat. Around 20 percent of the body's water comes from food (UCLA Health, 2022).

Here are some surprising foods and their approximate water content:

- Cucumber- 96%
- Iceberg lettuce- 96%
- Celery- 95%
- Radishes- 95%
- Romaine Lettuce- 95%
- Tomatoes- 94%
- Zucchini- 94%
- Bell peppers- 92%
- Cabbage- 92%
- Cauliflower- 92%
- Mushrooms- 92%
- Spinach- 92%
- Strawberries- 92%

Aside from the water content, these foods are packed with vitamins and minerals.

To get the most out of the water content, encourage your son to eat these foods raw. To make them more fun, you can make dips together to tickle their taste buds.

If you can add some avocado to your dip, that's an added bonus because it can also help the poop process.

TIPS FOR WIPING

As something that we do automatically, it's easy to forget that this is still a skill that little ones need to learn. You have two options: toilet paper or flushable wipes. Toilet paper is more convenient, and some toddlers prefer it over a wipe, which might be colder on the skin. On the other hand, it's easier for them to take a single wipe rather than having to pull off toilet roll and, inevitably, too much.

Show your son how to keep their hands flat for wiping. Explain how you wipe, then fold, then wipe again. If the wipe or paper is clean, they can throw it in the toilet. If not, they need to take another one and repeat the process. In the beginning, you may need to do the final wipe just to make sure your child is clean. Poop stains in underwear are not fun to wash and can be embarrassing for toddlers.

Even when parents aim to get everything right, there can be poop obstacles to overcome. In the next chapter, we will examine what can be done in these situations.

CHAPTER ELEVEN. POOP TRAINING HURDLES AND SPECIAL SCENARIOS

Considering the psychological and physiological differences between pee and poop, it's only natural that there might be a different set of challenges to overcome as toddlers master this particular skill. Constipation is a common concern, so we will begin by discussing this issue.

ADDRESSING RETENTION AND CONSTIPATION

Let's begin with a look at the constipation cycle. Poop builds up in the colon and starts to absorb water. Poop gets bigger, which makes it harder to pass, and this is what causes constipation in your son.

Eventually, the muscles in the rectum start to get tired because of the extra effort it takes to stretch. At the same time, the parts of the gut that recognize the need to poop also get tired.

Because of this, it gets harder to control poop. You may notice small amounts of softer, even liquid poop as accidents as it passes the hard poop in the colon.

Next in the constipation cycle are sensitive nerves in the gastrointestinal system, making the process more painful. This pain is why some children will intentionally hold their poop in, not to frustrate you but because of the discomfort or fear of pain.

Finally, tired muscles mean poop moves slower, and unfortunately, this only causes more constipation.

If you notice fear, a simple thing to try is to hug them while they are sitting on the potty or toilet or maybe hold their hand if that's enough to reassure them.

Nothing beats the loving arms of their favorite people, and this can be enough just to get past the first poop or two and overcome the initial fear.

A hug is a powerful stress reliever. During a hug, oxytocin is released, and this hormone not only decreases anxiety but also helps relieve pain!

There is one thing we have to clear up straight away. Adding more fiber to your son's diet is not necessarily the solution. Yes, fiber helps with the poop process, but too much fiber can actually lead to constipation because the body needs more fluids to absorb the extra fiber.

Here are some recipes that helped my little ones.

Wholemeal Toast with Almond Butter

Mix a teaspoon of ground flax with a tablespoon of almond butter and a tablespoon of applesauce. Instead of wholemeal toast, you can use anything that is wholemeal, such as waffles.

Spinach and Pear Smoothie

Blend 1 cup of baby spinach with 1 cup of pear juice, ½ cup of blueberries, and ½ cup of mango. You can also add a tablespoon of ground flax if you have some handy.

Oatmeal and Peanut Butter Balls

Add ½ cup of creamy peanut butter and ¼ cup of honey; warming gently. Add a cup of blended rolled oats. Mix the three ingredients together and then shape them into little balls.

Chocolate Avocado Pudding

Choose a soft, ripe avocado, peel it, and remove the pit. Put the avocado in a blender and add ½ cup of whole Greek yogurt, two tablespoons of cocoa powder, and two tablespoons of honey. Once blended into a smooth pudding, keep it in the fridge. It's quite rich, so they will only need a little bit at a time.

Coconut milk and oil are amazing constipation foods. Even a tablespoon of this oil can help toddlers with mild constipation. Try coconut oil and honey on toast, and replace your usual cooking oil with coconut oil. Coconut milk can be used as a base for smoothies and popsicles.

Hydration is even more crucial when your son is constipated. You will want to watch them drink, preferably from a spill-proof cup so that you can monitor closely how much they are taking in. Though they might not feel up to a run in the park, you still need to keep them active because this will also help with fluid intake. If drinking is a real challenge, think about offering rewards.

If you had a gassy baby, you may remember laying them on their backs as you moved their legs in a bicycle movement. This is still a good exercise to help with constipation. While in the same position, ask them to pull their knees into their chest to make themselves into a ball.

Sitting with their legs out straight, ask them to turn as far as they can to one side and then the other. Also, have them put their arms straight up in the air and lean to one side as you count to 10 and then again on the other side. All of these exercises will be easier and more fun if you do them together.

If you start to see behavioral problems, remember that it's most likely due to fear or pain. Remove any distractions that may have been used during toilet or potty time and wait until they calm down. Once they have settled, give them back their toy or book. It might take some time, but your patience is your best approach, which will pay off in the end.

HOW TO HELP RESOLVE DIARRHEA

Loose or watery poop, or diarrhea, can be acute or chronic. While acute diarrhea lasts a couple of days, chronic diarrhea can last for weeks and could be a sign of other health conditions, so you must see your doctor. Common causes of diarrhea include:

- Changes in the diet
- Too much fruit juice

- Infections
- Food intolerances/allergies
- Parasites
- Reactions to medicine

You might want to offer your son glucose-electrolyte solutions because they have the right balance of water, sugar, and salts. Baked potatoes and meats are a good place to start as well as pasta, white rice, white bread, and cereals. These foods will help bind the poop. Unlike with constipation, cooked vegetables and eggs can also help. What may surprise you is that unripe bananas are good for diarrhea because of the higher levels of resistant starch, whereas ripe bananas can have a better effect on constipation.

Whether it's diarrhea or constipation, if you see any blood in your toddler's poo, please see a doctor straight away!

POOP REGRESSION

Dealing with poop regression is very similar to pee regression, and the first step is to work out what could be the cause of the stress your little one is going through. The only difference is that you may have to consider whether constipation or diarrhea is causing the problem. Past negative experiences, not just pain and fear but also shame, could cause your son to go back to having more accidents than before.

When this happened with my son, I went back to sitting on the bathroom floor for a few moments to try and see things from his point of view and discover if anything had changed. We had conversations about whether anything was worrying him or if there were any changes at daycare that I might have missed. After ruling out all other reasons, I decided the poop regression may have been due to our relaxation of routine and reminders. And to be honest, my potty dances had become less enthusiastic.

I decided to change the rewards. It was as simple as getting new stickers because my son's favorite cartoon character changed. We then went back to a stricter routine of me reminding him to sit on the potty during the day, and then at certain times when I knew he had due to poop, I wouldn't remind him, but I would say, "Let's go and sit on the potty." Reminders are good, but sometimes, asking if they want to go will lead to a no because they would rather be doing other things.

What to Do When Your Son Poops in Bed

The simplest solution to this problem is to consider whether they eat dinner too late. Ideally, toddlers should have dinner at least two or three hours before bed. We all know this isn't always practical and they may ask for a snack between dinner and bed. In this case, offering a snack high in the amino acid called tryptophan is best. Tryptophan turns into serotonin, which then produces the sleep hormone melatonin. The last thing you want is an energized toddler at bedtime, which could throw your routine out the window. Nuts and seeds, cheese, turkey, oats, and eggs are high in tryptophan, but remember to keep the portion small.

Of course, if bedtime pooping is the problem, snacks aren't going to help. To gauge whether they need a snack before bed, monitor their appetite in the morning. The bedtime snack might be unnecessary if you notice they are losing interest in breakfast.

It's important not to offer your son his favorite food as a snack before bedtime. There are two reasons for this. You don't want to see this snack as some kind of bribe and, secondly, they may stop eating all of their dinner knowing they will get something "better" later on. This can lead to an unhealthy relationship with food and even using food for emotional comfort or overeating.

An alternative would be to offer a small glass of milk at least an hour before bed. Toddlers can often confuse hunger with thirst, especially as the body cues are subtle. Though there are separate neurons in the brain for thirst and hunger, the messages are in the same part of the brain. Many adults will eat instead of drinking, so it's only normal for a toddler to mix these signals up. If a toddler is thirsty, the aching in their tummy will disappear after a drink. If they are hungry, it will remain. It's a good idea to put this into practice at other times of the day. This helps ensure that you are both more aware of whether it's hunger or thirst.

The final toilet trip before bed should be more of a "Let's sit on the" potty as part of their routine rather than a reminder! If pooping in bed is a problem, you may need to encourage them to sit for a little longer, especially if you haven't seen a poop for a while.

This phase isn't going to last forever and how you react can make bedtime pooping last longer than it needs to. Accidents are going to happen, but adjusting your child's dinner and bedtime routine can help. After that, it's down to a bit of patience on your behalf.

Toddlers are smart little creatures, and in the kindest possible way, they know how to play us! Bedtimes can be as notoriously difficult as potty training, with numerous attempts to get your attention when they should be sleeping. It's not to say that they are pooping in bed on purpose, but they may still be seeking your attention.

If they have an accident in bed, make the cleanup process as calm as possible. You may still have the nighttime supplies from when you first removed the diaper; if not, get them back out again. Try to keep the lights as dim as possible, with minimal fuss change, followed by a kiss and "goodnight." The more attention you give them, the more likely the habit will continue.

Poop Smearing: Don't Panic!

Now, there is one potential problem that no parent wants to discuss, mainly because, for adults, it can seem like a worrying and even disgusting habit, but I promise you aren't alone. I'm talking about poop smearing, a behavior when toddlers smear their poop on anything. From a parent's point of view, it can be heartbreaking for your little one to call you and discover a room like this, and naturally, your mind is going to start thinking the worst.

Let's get the biggest fear over with. Poop smearing may indeed be a sign of psychological issues and processing differences seen in conditions like autism and ADHD and cases of trauma or depression. But you need to remember that poop smearing is one symptom and not a diagnosis. It may also just be that they have a stomachache or are constipated and have accidentally touched their poop and wiped their hands on anything nearby. If you think it's medical or psychological, it's worth talking to your doctor.

Next, this habit could be because of behavioral issues, and it goes back to the need for any form of attention. Again, this isn't something to be concerned about straight away. The difference between an accident and smearing is that they are looking for a reaction from you, so your response to the situation has to be even more minimal. Try to use as few words as possible and limit eye contact as long as you are sure this is a cry for attention and have ruled out other potential reasons for the smearing. Also, consider how you are cleaning them up. For some, a nice warm bath rather than being in bed can be a reward, so you may want to shower them instead.

Finally, it could be a sensory issue. Young children use their senses to explore the world. If they aren't getting enough sensory stimulus during the day, they may take opportunities to explore in bed, and unfortunately for you, this means exploring their poop!

Try increasing sensory stimulation during playtime before panicking about other reasons for this behavior. This could be as simple as getting a tray and squirting shaving foam in it, hiding some toys and letting them find them, or adding drops of food coloring so they can explore the changing colors.

Flour and water are another good choice, especially if you add a few drops of essential oils or just finger painting. Yes, it will be messy, but it's better to clean up a ton of paint and flour than poop all over the walls!

It might be more difficult for your son to poop in other people's houses at first, and there are endless reasons for this, all of which could have been the same stressors that were once a problem in your own home. The lighting may be off, the smells are different, they aren't comfortable sitting on a toilet when they are used to their potty, or they may find it harder to relax.

Even if your child is happily going to the bathroom by themselves in your home, it's worth going with them when visiting friends and relatives. Keep an eye on the time. It's easy to get lost in conversation and forget that it's usually the time your little one wants a poop. Stick to the same routine even if you are away from home. For instance, if it's before a meal and you normally tell them to sit on the potty, continue doing so. Then, remind them to ask you if they need the potty at the same regular intervals as they would on any other day.

Don't feel like the weird parent who takes the potty or travel seat with them everywhere they go. If others want to judge your dedication to your child, so be it. Peeing in someone else's toilet may be more difficult for your child and holding in poop can cause serious problems. So, if carrying that Spiderman potty with you prevents constipation, that's the way to go!

If your son is at daycare, you will probably have already communicated certain potty-training techniques you have been using. Nevertheless, updates and changes should be communicated, including changes in diet and any incidences of holding in, constipation, or regression. If your child has any additional needs, be sure that the daycare is accommodating for them.

Traveling and holidays can create mixed emotions for toddlers, and as excited as we are for a change of scenery, it can be nerve-wracking for a little person. Aside from completely shaking up their routine, being in new places can be a bit intimidating, especially when using unfamiliar bathrooms.

If you happen to be traveling when there is a risk for accidents, it's a good idea to avoid hotels at first and perhaps go for an Airbnb or similar and plan to stay there for a few days if possible. This way, you have access to a washing machine and don't end up attempting to wash poop out of clothes in hotel bathrooms. Pack extra plastic bags for times when washing machines aren't available. Also, time in one place can help them gain some confidence and relax enough to poop.

Finally, flying with a toddler can be the most terrifying because it's hard for them to understand that when the seatbelt light is on, there is no chance of going to the toilet. The best thing is to limit snacks and fluids before the flight. As you need to be at the airport at least two hours before the flight, it's a good rule of thumb to use this time to focus on emptying rather than filling them up. If you have the option to choose your seat, aim for one close to the toilets and an aisle seat for quick access.

Wherever you plan to go, whether for a few days or a few weeks, try to incorporate elements of your child's usual routine. For example, if they sit on the potty before meals or a bath, do the same when you are away and don't forget to take your rewards system with you.

HELPING TODDLERS ADAPT TO CHANGE

If there is one general theme that you may have noticed, it's that routine and relaxation are crucial when it comes to managing poop issues. Stress can quickly cause many of the poop problems, which is why we have been making every effort to avoid them. In this final section, we will discover how to help toddlers manage change and develop resilience. While it may seem like a lot for a little person, it's a life skill that will serve them well.

You can't expect every day to go the same way according to your routine. Someone could get sick, one parent may need to go away for work, and a host of other things can put a spanner in the works. To help prevent distress, try to keep as many aspects of their usual routine the same.

Personally, mealtimes are one of those things that I find important, in particular, for poop! At the same time, if something has interrupted your routine, it's perfectly normal not to be able to cook the nutritious meal you had planned. My tip is always to have a couple of toddler portion meals in the freezer for days like this. Making sure meals are on time means the rest of the evening routine remains on track and they will be in bed on time.

How you handle changes to the routine can reflect on your son. It's unrealistic for you to breeze through life without stress affecting you but when possible, take a breath, walk away from your son, let out your frustrations, and return once you have calmed down. Give them a positive example when it comes to handling changes to routines and the stresses they cause.

For the more significant changes, like moving house, try to avoid surprises. Surprises are a little bit like vacations: we might like them, but for a toddler, they can just cause more upset than joy. Instead, ask your son for help and give them chances to assert their mini authority through choices. Ask them if they want to help put their toys in boxes and which box they think would be good to use. They could even be in charge of color-coding boxes for different rooms in the house. You might be tempted to do as much as possible when they aren't around but arriving home one day and seeing their entire room packed up or all their toys gone will terrify them, even make them feel like they are being punished.

Change can be helped a lot by social stories and preempting any potential concerns they might have. Keep up the conversations with your son and practice active listening when discussing their feelings and worries.

Poop never gets enough attention, like it's part of potty training that just occurs naturally once pee is mastered, but many toddlers need additional support. And even then, on some rare occasions, nothing seems to work. In our penultimate chapter, we will discover what needs to be done when this is the case.

CHAPTER TWELVE. WHAT HAPPENS WHEN NOTHING WORKS

If there is one thing I thank the lucky stars for, it's that all of my children were born healthy, and although potty training was more challenging than many other parents' experiences, there were no major health concerns. Not everyone can say the same.

FREDDIE'S STORY

This wasn't the case for Megan and William. Their son Freddie was born at 34 weeks and needed to be on antibiotics for an infection. This played havoc on his tiny digestive system, something that bothered him his whole infant life, mainly with constipation. That being said, there were no developmental delays or disorders, and Megan and William felt Freddie was showing signs of readiness just after his second birthday.

They felt the 3-day method was suitable for them, so they did all the necessary research, got the supplies, and began introducing Freddie to the concept of the potty. Most importantly, they chose a time when Freddie's constipation wasn't causing him any problems. The rewards were ready, the stories had been told, and everyone woke up on day 1 almost excited.

There was no success on day 1, but neither parent was disheartened. There was also no success on day 2, so they decided to try bottomless instead of underwear and kept their levels of enthusiasm and positivity high. Yet on day 2, there was still not even a drop of pee in the potty. Megan thought the rewards weren't exciting enough, and there was still day 3 to go.

But on day 3, things felt like they were going backward. Freddie was happy to sit on the potty, but 10 minutes later, he would pee on the floor. The biggest problem was that Freddie was holding in his poop, and the parents both knew that this was going to only add to Freddie's psychological problems regarding poop.

Megan and Freddie had to face the fact that even though Freddie was communicating his needs, he wasn't emotionally ready for potty training. Initially, they were concerned that not continuing would send mixed signals, and it felt like they had all failed. William explained to Freddie that it wasn't his fault and they would try again another time.

As a parent or caregiver of a toddler, you need to decide when pushing the potty-training process does more harm than good. Only you can tell if another day will make the difference or whether your son has something going on in his mind that will prevent any success.

There shouldn't be any fear of delaying potty training or concerns that their development is going to suffer. Remember when your son took their first steps before falling to the floor? Then think about the difference a month made. In these crucial years, children develop so quickly that it may just be a matter of weeks before you can try again.

THE SECOND ATTEMPT

Three weeks after their first attempt, Freddie came up to his parents and told them that his diaper was wet. They decided to take the potty out again without making too much fuss and leave it in a visible place.

On the first day of going bottomless with the potty in view, Megan and William offered gentle reminders that it was there if he wanted to try and sit on it, and that same day, they were able to do the potty dance with the first pee in the potty.

Poop was still a problem. Past experiences of constipation were playing on Freddie's mind, and even after two weeks of successfully peeing in the potty, every poop was an accident.

This tested Megan and William's patience to the limit, and deep down, they knew Freddie could feel the disappointment. He became withdrawn and sad, and accidents with pee started to happen.

This is why a parent's mentality is pivotal. There is nothing worse than recycled advice, but when it comes with scientific evidence, it suddenly makes sense.

HOW TO STAY CALM WHEN POOP IS ALL OVER THE FLOOR

When you are stressed and anxious, your sympathetic nervous system kicks in. This is the part of the nervous system that controls the fight or flight response. Your heart rate increases, breathing becomes rapid, and even digestion is suppressed. In order to relax again, your parasympathetic nervous system (or the rest and digest response) needs to be activated to create a balance within the body. Bear in mind that depending on the stressor, it can take the body 20 to 30 minutes to return to a calm state.

There is an amazing nerve in your body called the vagus nerve. It's the 10th cranial nerve and means *wandering* in Latin because it begins at the base of the brain, passes your vocal cords, meanders down the body, branching into the heart, lungs, and all the way down to the gut. The vagus nerve contains anywhere from 75 percent to 90 percent of your parasympathetic nervous system's nerve fibers. Stimulating this miracle nerve can help send the necessary messages between the brain, heart, and digestive system to calm down.

Taking deep breaths may sound like an old wives' tale but it works because it stimulates the vagus nerve! Other ways to help your vagus nerve include splashing cold water on your face (also not an old wives' tale). Or you could try singing or humming because the vagus nerve passes your vocal cords.

If at any stage you feel your emotions are getting the better of you, you need to walk away. Even if that means you leave your son with a baby wipe to attempt to clean himself for two minutes. It's not cruel because it will have a positive impact on potty training sooner than you imagine.

Megan and William went back to square one with their potty training and added some much-needed calming techniques. In order to help Freddie overcome his fear of pooping, his parents played videos of animals pooping. They encouraged him into the bathroom when they were going to show how it isn't always a painful experience. Monitoring the times Freddie would normally poop, they sat him on the toilet with the videos.

After a couple of days, Freddie was back to no pee accidents, and within a week, poop was going in the potty! Patience and perseverance are your winning tools when nothing else seems to work!

As we wrap up, let's gather all our tools and resources to reinforce the 3-day potty training method for boys and cement your family's success!

CHAPTER THIRTEEN. RESOURCES AND TOOLS FOR CONTINUED TRIUMPH

Let's begin with a perfect summary of the 3-day potty training for boys with this complete checklist for your progress!

Scan the QR code to get checklist on your phone.

BEFORE STARTING

✓ Introduce your chosen vocabulary and normalize pee and poop

✓ Use books and visual cues to explain the process

✓ Pay attention to verbal signs that your son might be using

✓ Look for physical signs of readiness

✓ Gather your supplies

✓ Consider the reward system you want to use

✓ Set up your bathroom for success

✓ Talk to everyone involved in your son's life for consistency

✓ Begin practicing useful skills like pushing down pants

DAY 1

✓ Start your day in the most positive way

✓ Take your son straight to the potty when they wake up

✓ Stick to your routine

✓ Make sure your son is encouraged to stay hydrated

✓ Give them choices for independence

✓ Remind them to sit on the potty

✓ Stay calm during the expected accidents

✓ Don't use phrases like "It's okay." Let them know they can try again next time

✓ Celebrate any success, even if it's a dribble of pee, after you have carried them

✓ Enjoy five minutes to reflect and check that your expectations are realistic

DAY 2

✓ Start the day positively. Reflect on what you learned from day 1

✓ Stick to the same routine as day 1

✓ Double-check your levels of enthusiasm

✓ Praise any signs of independence, such as sitting on the potty without reminders

✓ Practice your relaxation techniques and remain calm

✓ Be consistent with your rewards

✓ Consider a bigger reward, such as choosing dinner, for bigger successes

DAY 3

✓ Begin the day by considering if any changes need to be made

✓ Keep to the same routine for potty reminders

✓ If progress is being made, consider a short trip out

✓ If there are behavioral issues, think of the reasons and solutions

✓ Encourage more independence, ask them what step comes next

✓ Prepare for daycare or other caregivers your son might spend time with

✓ Don't give up on positive reinforcement, praise, and celebrations

POST DAY 3

✓ Keep a bag of wipes, a plastic bag, and clean clothes ready for going out

✓ Rule out any medical issues if you suspect problems

✓ Integrate your potty training routine into normal days

✓ Continue to communicate updates and changes with caregivers

✓ Look out for signs of nighttime readiness

✓ Address potty-training regression as quickly as possible

✓ Gradually reduce your rewards when accidents are rare

POTTY TRAINING REWARD CHART

Here are some sites that offer **free downloadable** potty-training charts (you can find all direct links in the checklist):

- *Elmo Potty Training Chart*
- *Dino Potty Training Chart*
- *Super Simple Potty Training Chart*

You can also make your own or copy the example I used with my boys.

APPS FOR TRACKING AND LEARNING VIDEOS

In a digital world, it makes sense that there are dozens of apps that can help you keep track of pee and poop and even where they go! Below are some of my favorites:

- ***Potty Whiz**, The Potty Training App*
- *Daniel Tiger's* ***Stop & Go Potty***
- ***Potty Time***

They are available for Apple, too.

A quick internet search will result in more options, and the same can be said for **videos** that help explain the potty-training process. Again, here are a few to get you started:

- *Peppa Pig Learns How To Use A Potty*
- *Pirate Pete's Potty | Potty Training Video For Toddlers*

- *POCOYO ENGLISH - Potty Training - Potty Song*
- *Potty Training with Steve and Maggie*
- *Daniel Tiger 🚽 Potty Training*

VISUAL CUES FOR POTTY TRAINING

Aside from taking photos of the process to help your son, you can also use any of the following sites (search on Google or find links in the checklist) to download and print visual cues to support all toddlers, especially those who are non-verbal:

- *Visual Timetable Using the Toilet (Boys)*
- *Toileting Picture Cards*
- *Toileting Sequence Visual Supports*
- *Potty Training Tips for Children with Autism*

Makaton Toilet Routine

If you are interested in learning Makaton signs to support the potty-training process, I found the following Youtube video to be very practical:

- *Makaton Toilet Routine Video*

Sign Language

If you are teaching your child sign language, be sure to find the signs for your particular country, as they may vary.

Here is an example of American sign language and potty-training words on Youtube.

- *10 ASL Bathroom Signs to Teach Your Baby & Toddler*

FINDING SUPPORT

The great news about online support is that you have a world of parental experiences and experts to hear from without leaving your home. The resources below are a mixture of expert advice, consultancy services, and forums:

- The Potty School
- ERIC.org
- Potty Training Consultant
- Little Ones at Home
- The Bump Forum
- What to Expect Forum
- Family Lives Forum

At first, you might feel a little awkward joining a forum, but there is a huge sense of relief when you can share your story and experiences, knowing that there are parents who aren't judging because they are going through similar experiences.

Every child's journey is unique, and every victory, regardless of how small, is monumental. And if success isn't as fast as you had hoped, relax because it will happen!

CONCLUSION

Nobody said parenting was easy, but let's face it, few people are there to remind you that it's also the best and most rewarding experience a human can go through. Nothing beats the unconditional love you receive from these little people and their genuine excitement when they achieve something. And through all of the pee and poop cleaning, it's those moments of joy on their face that remind you that it's all worth it!

While potty training is a particularly challenging time, there is no need to make it more difficult than it should be. If you are in any way concerned about your son's health or development (physical, mental, or emotional), it's best to seek the right medical advice before potty training, and this often starts with your family doctor or pediatrician. You will be able to get the necessary support for your family before attempting to potty train. Regarding children, it's always better to be safe than sorry!

For me, it was important to recognize this stage of my sons' lives in two parts: the physical aspects of potty training and the emotional side for the whole family.

In terms of the physical aspects, preparation is key. You need to be able to recognize their individual signs of readiness and work on communication, whether verbal or nonverbal. It's also essential to get your son involved in choosing your supplies to keep them motivated. There is no point starting with a boring blue potty if they are just going to refuse to sit on it. This will only result in you having to find another solution and additional expenses.

When it comes to emotional preparation, this is just a task for you as it is for them. They need to be emotionally prepared, which involves getting down on their level and appreciating that their fears or concerns are real. More often than not, fears can be overcome with social stories and sensory adjustments. The goal before success with the potty has to be to overcome fears so that your son is relaxed.

For the behavioral issue, you can't afford for emotions to get in the way and a power struggle to begin. If there are any stressors in the family's life, it's best to resolve these first. I swear, at one point, my son looked me in the eye and released a giant poop on the floor just to see my reaction. He seemed disappointed when I walked away, danced it out in the next room, and came back as if nothing had boiled my anger.

If you need help managing those emotions, and there is absolutely no shame in this, I found the book *Anger*

Management for Parents to help with the many challenges parenting can bring.

Positivity is the power you need, and if it's anything less than genuine, your son will see right through you. Don't forget that when it comes to rewards, start small. You will be amazed when you find that your cheers of celebration and warm hugs are enough to start the ball rolling. You will always then have other rewards to fall back on if the love and warmth aren't enough.

The 3-day potty training method for boys is intense and not just in learning. You will probably have had a rollercoaster of emotions through the ups and downs, and this will continue in your journey beyond this point. There will be accidents to clean up calmly, and there will be plenty more celebrations, such as dry nights and fully mastering the control of their bowel movements. New fears may arise, and these will require a little retraining, but the results are always moving toward greater independence.

There may be times when you can't see the light of day, but I promise, you've got this. Patience, perseverance, and positivity will lead you to potty-trained little boys, independence, and another life skill mastered! Good luck!

A SHORT MESSAGE FROM THE AUTHOR

Would You Kindly Share Your Thoughts?

Thank you for reading "Potty Training for Boys"!

If you could spare a few moments to leave a review, it would mean the world to me and greatly assist potential readers in discovering and enjoying this book.

Your honest opinion, even if it's a couple of words, makes a significant difference.

As a small author, your feedback is incredibly valuable. Reviews from readers like you not only help me grow and improve as a writer but also play a crucial role in supporting and giving visibility to my work.

Scan the QR code below to leave a quick review

Thank you so much for your support!

Warm regards,

Jane

REFERENCES

15 Foods That Help You Stay Hydrated. (2022, June 17). Retrieved from https://www.uclahealth.org/news/15-food-that-help-you-stay-hydrated

Allied Services Integrated Health. (2020, June 23). The vagus nerve: your secret weapon in fighting stress. Retrieved from https://www.allied-services.org/news/2020/june/the-vagus-nerve-your-secret-weapon-in-fighting-s/

Arky, B. (2023, October 30). Sensory processing issues explained. Retrieved from https://childmind.org/article/sensory-processing-issues-explained/#

Coucouvanis, J. A. (2008). *The Potty Journey: Guide to Toilet Training Children with Special Needs, Including Autism and Related Disorders*. Autism Asperger Publishing Company.

Dewar, G. (2022, March 13). Potty training tips: An evidence-based guide for the thinking parent. Retrieved from https://parentingscience.com/potty-training-tips/

Emotional issues and potty training problems. (n.d.). Retrieved from https://www.healthychildren.org/English/ages-stages/toddler/toilet-training/Pages/Emotional-Issues-and-Bathroom-Problems.aspx

Forehand, R., & Long, N. (2010). *Parenting the Strong-Willed Child: The Clinically Proven Five-Week Program for Parents of Two- to Six-Year-Olds*. McGraw-Hill Education.

Glowacki, J. (2015). *Oh Crap! Potty Training: Everything Modern Parents Need to Know to Do It Once and Do It Right*. Touchstone.

Grant, B. (2022, September 28). Smearing - ERIC. Retrieved from https://eric.org.uk/smearing/

Herrmann, S., MD. (2023, June 14). Q&A: Constipation in children. Retrieved from https://www.mayoclinichealthsystem.org/hometown-health/speaking-of-health/qa-constipation-in-children#:

Howard, J. (2017, November 8). How the World Potty Trains. Retrieved from https://edition.cnn.com/2017/10/31/health/potty-training-parenting-without-borders-explainer/index.html

Kiddoo, D. (2012). Toilet Training Children: When to Start and How to Train. *Canadian Medical Association Journal, 184*(5), 511. https://doi.org/10.1503/cmaj.110830

Lekovic, J. M. (2006). *Diaper-Free Before 3: The Healthier Way to Toilet Train and Help Your Child Out of Diapers Sooner*. Crown.

Medical Home Portal - Toilet Training Children with Complex Medical Conditions. (n.d.). Retrieved from https://www.medicalhomeportal.org/clinical-practice/common-issues-for-cyshcn/toilet-training-children-with-complex-medical-conditions

Nall, R. N. M. (2018, September 7). Shy bladder (Paruresis). Retrieved from https://www.healthline.com/health/shy-bladder#:

NHS. (2023, May 18). How to Potty Train. Retrieved from *https://www.nhs.uk/conditions/baby/babys-development/potty-training-and-bedwetting/how-to-potty-train/*

Smarter potty training. (2023, May 3). Retrieved from https://www.constipationcoach.com/blogs/news/smarter-potty-training

Toilet training. (2019, December 26). Retrieved from https://www.hopkinsmedicine.org/health/wellness-and-prevention/toilettraining

Vethavanam, V. (2023, February 28). Potty training boys is harder than girls - revealed! Retrieved from https://www.-madeformums.com/toddler-and-preschool/potty-training-boys-is-harder-than-girls-revealed/

Made in United States
Orlando, FL
28 May 2024